MCP Mathematics

Richard Monnard • Royce Hargrove

Copyright © 2005 by Pearson Education, Inc., publishing as Dale Seymour Publications®, an imprint of Pearson Learning Group, 299 Jefferson Road, Parsippany, NJ 07054. All rights reserved. No part of this book may be reproduced or transmitted in any form or by any means, electronic or mechanical, including photocopying, recording, or by any information storage and retrieval system, without permission in writing from the publisher. For information regarding permission(s), write to Rights and Permissions Department.

Dale Seymour Publications® is a registered trademark of Dale Seymour Publications, Inc.

ISBN 0-7652-6058-1
Printed in the United States of America
14   16

Project Staff	
Art & Design:	Robert Dobaczewski, Kathleen Ellison, Senja Lauderdale, David Mager, Jim O'Shea, Angel Weyant
Editorial:	Stephanie P. Cahill, Gina Dalessio, Phyllis Dunsay, Mary Ellen Gilbert, Dena Kennedy, Theresa McCarthy, Marilyn Sarch
Marketing:	Doug Falk, Clare Harrison
Production/Manufacturing:	Irene Belinsky, Lawrence Berkowitz, Louis Campos, Diane Fristachi, Pamela Gallo, Leslie Greenberg, Suellen Leavy, Ruth Leine, Karyn Mueller, Michele Uhl
Publishing Operations:	Carolyn Coyle, Richetta Lobban

1-800-321-3106
www.pearsonlearning.com

Contents

Chapter 1 — Basic Facts Through 10

Lesson 1-1	Numbers 0 Through 10	1
Lesson 1-2	Sums Through 5	3
Lesson 1-3	Sums Through 10	5
Lesson 1-4	Subtracting From 5 and Less	7
Lesson 1-5	Subtracting From 10 and Less	9
Lesson 1-6	Mixed Practice	11
Lesson 1-7	**Problem Solving:** Write a Number Sentence *It's Algebra!*	13
	Chapter 1 Test	15

Chapter 2 — Basic Facts Through 12

Lesson 2-1	Sums Through 12	17
Lesson 2-2	Practice Sums Through 12	19
Lesson 2-3	**Problem Solving:** Make and Use a Table	21
Lesson 2-4	Subtracting From 12 and Less	23
Lesson 2-5	Practice Subtracting From 12 and Less	25
Lesson 2-6	Mixed Practice	27
Lesson 2-7	**Problem Solving:** Act It Out	29
	Chapter 2 Test	31
	Cumulative Assessment	32

Chapter 3 — Addition Facts Through 18

Lesson 3-1	Numbers Through 19	33
Lesson 3-2	Review Sums Through 12	35
Lesson 3-3	Sums Through 14	37
Lesson 3-4	Money Sums Through 14¢	39
Lesson 3-5	Sums Through 16	41
Lesson 3-6	Sums Through 18	43
Lesson 3-7	Column Addition *It's Algebra!*	45
Lesson 3-8	Money Sums Through 18¢	47
Lesson 3-9	**Problem Solving:** Too Much Information	49
	Chapter 3 Test	51
	Cumulative Assessment	52

Chapter 4 — Subtraction Facts Through 18

Lesson 4-1	Review Subtracting From 12 and Less	53
Lesson 4-2	Subtracting From 14 and Less	55
Lesson 4-3	**Problem Solving:** Make and Use a Line Plot	57

Lesson 4-4	Subtracting From 16 and Less 59
Lesson 4-5	Subtracting From 18 and Less 61
Lesson 4-6	Practice Subtracting From 18 and Less 63
Lesson 4-7	Subtracting From 18¢ and Less 65
	Chapter 4 Test 67
	● **Cumulative Assessment** 68

Chapter 5 — Numbers Through Hundreds

Lesson 5-1	Numbers Through 100 69
Lesson 5-2	Counting Hundreds, Tens, and Ones 71
Lesson 5-3	Place Value Through Hundreds 73
Lesson 5-4	Counting Dollars, Dimes, and Pennies 75
Lesson 5-5	Counting Through 1,000 77
Lesson 5-6	10 More, 10 Less; 100 More, 100 Less 79
Lesson 5-7	Comparing 2-Digit Numbers *It's Algebra!* 81
Lesson 5-8	Comparing 3-Digit Numbers *It's Algebra!* 83
Lesson 5-9	Ordinal Numbers 85
Lesson 5-10	Number Names 87
Lesson 5-11	● **Problem Solving:** Look for a Pattern 89
	Chapter 5 Test 91
	● **Cumulative Assessment** 92

Chapter 6 — Time and Money

Lesson 6-1	Telling Time to the Hour and Half-Hour 93
Lesson 6-2	Telling Time to 5 Minutes 95
Lesson 6-3	Telling Time, Before and After 97
Lesson 6-4	Elapsed Time 99
Lesson 6-5	Telling Time to the Minute 101
Lesson 6-6	Days, Weeks, and Months 103
Lesson 6-7	Using a Calendar 105
Lesson 6-8	Counting Money Through Dimes 107
Lesson 6-9	Counting Money Through Quarters 109
Lesson 6-10	Counting Money Through Half-Dollars 111
Lesson 6-11	Counting Money Through Dollars 113
Lesson 6-12	● **Problem Solving:** Act It Out 115
	Chapter 6 Test 117
	● **Cumulative Assessment** 118
	Math Transition Award 119

Chapter 7 — Addition With 2-Digit Numbers

Lesson 7-1	Adding 2-Digit and 1-Digit Numbers	121
Lesson 7-2	Addition With Regrouping	123
Lesson 7-3	Adding 2-Digit Numbers	125
Lesson 7-4	Adding Multiples of 10	127
Lesson 7-5	Finding 3-Digit Sums	129
Lesson 7-6	Adding Money	131
Lesson 7-7	• **Problem Solving:** Make an Organized List	133
	Chapter 7 Test	135
	• **Cumulative Assessment**	136

Chapter 8 — Subtraction With 2-Digit Numbers

Lesson 8-1	Subtracting 2-Digit Numbers	137
Lesson 8-2	Regrouping a Ten to Subtract	139
Lesson 8-3	Subtracting With Regrouping	141
Lesson 8-4	Review Subtracting With Regrouping	143
Lesson 8-5	Practice Subtracting With Regrouping	145
Lesson 8-6	Using Addition to Check Subtraction	147
Lesson 8-7	Subtracting Money	149
Lesson 8-8	• **Problem Solving:** Make and Use a Graph	151
	Chapter 8 Test	153
	• **Cumulative Assessment**	154

Chapter 9 — Adding and Subtracting 2-Digit Numbers

Lesson 9-1	Finding 2- or 3-Digit Sums	155
Lesson 9-2	Column Addition *It's Algebra!*	157
Lesson 9-3	Subtracting With Regrouping	159
Lesson 9-4	Mixed Review	161
Lesson 9-5	Addition and Subtraction Sentences	163
Lesson 9-6	Subtracting Money	165
Lesson 9-7	Adding Money	167
Lesson 9-8	Estimating Sums *It's Algebra!*	169
Lesson 9-9	• **Problem Solving:** Choose an Operation	171
	Chapter 9 Test	173
	• **Cumulative Assessment**	174

Chapter 10 — Adding 3-Digit Numbers

Lesson 10-1	Place Value Through 1,000	175
Lesson 10-2	Review Adding 2-Digit Numbers	177
Lesson 10-3	Adding a 3-Digit and a 1-Digit Number	179
Lesson 10-4	Adding a 3-Digit and a 2-Digit Number	181

Lesson 10-5	Adding With 2 Regroupings	183
Lesson 10-6	Practice Adding with 1 or 2 Regroupings	185
Lesson 10-7	Adding Two 3-Digit Numbers	187
Lesson 10-8	Adding 3-Digit Numbers	189
Lesson 10-9	Adding Money	191
Lesson 10-10	Estimating Cost **It's Algebra!**	193
Lesson 10-11	• **Problem Solving:** Use Information From a List	195
	Chapter 10 Test	197
	• **Cumulative Assessment**	198

Chapter 11 Subtracting 3-Digit Numbers

Lesson 11-1	Subtracting a 1-Digit From a 2-Digit Number	199
Lesson 11-2	Subtracting 2-Digit Numbers	201
Lesson 11-3	Subtracting a 1-Digit From a 3-Digit Number	203
Lesson 11-4	Subtracting Multiples of 10	205
Lesson 11-5	Subtracting a 2-Digit From a 3-Digit Number	207
Lesson 11-6	Subtracting 3-Digit Numbers	209
Lesson 11-7	Practice Subtracting With 1 or 2 Regroupings	211
Lesson 11-8	Subtracting Money	213
Lesson 11-9	Estimating Differences **It's Algebra!**	215
Lesson 11-10	• **Problem Solving:** Use Logical Reasoning **It's Algebra!**	217
	Chapter 11 Test	219
	• **Cumulative Assessment**	220

Chapter 12 Adding and Subtracting 3-Digit Numbers

Lesson 12-1	Adding 3-Digit Numbers	221
Lesson 12-2	Column Addition **It's Algebra!**	223
Lesson 12-3	Subtracting 3-Digit Numbers	225
Lesson 12-4	Practice Subtracting 3-Digit Numbers	227
Lesson 12-5	Checking Subtraction	229
Lesson 12-6	Subtracting Money	231
Lesson 12-7	• **Problem Solving:** Use Data From a Picture	233
	Chapter 12 Test	235
	• **Cumulative Assessment**	236

Chapter 13 Geometry and Fractions

Lesson 13-1	Solid Figures	237
Lesson 13-2	Faces, Vertices, and Edges	239
Lesson 13-3	Plane Figures	241
Lesson 13-4	Slides, Flips, and Turns	243
Lesson 13-5	Symmetry	245
Lesson 13-6	Fractions	247

Lesson 13-7	Fractional Parts 249
Lesson 13-8	Parts of a Whole 251
Lesson 13-9	Parts of a Group With the Same Objects 253
Lesson 13-10	Parts of a Group With Different Objects 255
Lesson 13-11	● **Problem Solving:** Draw a Picture 257
	Chapter 13 Test 259
	● **Cumulative Assessment** 260

Chapter 14 — Measurement

Lesson 14-1	Inches and Feet 261
Lesson 14-2	Measuring to the Nearest Inch 263
Lesson 14-3	Pounds and Ounces 265
Lesson 14-4	Cups, Pints, and Quarts 267
Lesson 14-5	Centimeters and Meters 269
Lesson 14-6	Measuring to the Nearest Centimeter 271
Lesson 14-7	Grams and Kilograms 273
Lesson 14-8	Milliliters and Liters 275
Lesson 14-9	Perimeter 277
Lesson 14-10	● **Problem Solving:** Try, Check, and Revise *It's Algebra!* 279
Lesson 14-11	Area 281
Lesson 14-12	Temperature 283
	Chapter 14 Test 285
	● **Cumulative Assessment** 286

Chapter 15 — Multiplication and Division Through 5

Lesson 15-1	Multiplying by the Factor 2 287
Lesson 15-2	Multiplying by the Factor 3 289
Lesson 15-3	Multiplying by the Factor 4 291
Lesson 15-4	Multiplying by the Factor 5 293
Lesson 15-5	Order in Multiplication 295
Lesson 15-6	● **Problem Solving:** Choose an Operation *It's Algebra!* 297
Lesson 15-7	Dividing by 2 *It's Algebra!* 299
Lesson 15-8	Dividing by 3 *It's Algebra!* 301
Lesson 15-9	Dividing by 4 *It's Algebra!* 303
Lesson 15-10	Dividing by 5 *It's Algebra!* 305
Lesson 15-11	● **Problem Solving:** Make and Use a Picture Graph 307
Lesson 15-12	Coordinate Graph *It's Algebra!* 309
	Chapter 15 Test 311
	● **Cumulative Assessment** 312

Glossary 313

Name _____

Basic Facts Through 10

Chapter 1

Lesson 1-1

Match the set to the number.
Match the number to the number name.

1	two
9	one
2	four
4	nine
3	ten
0	five
10	three
5	zero
7	seven
8	six
6	eight

Lesson 1-1 • Numbers 0 Through 10

one 1

Write the numbers.

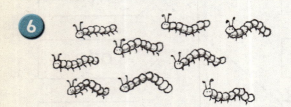 

 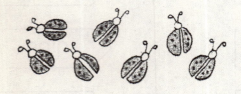 

    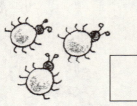

12 Connect the dots.

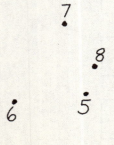 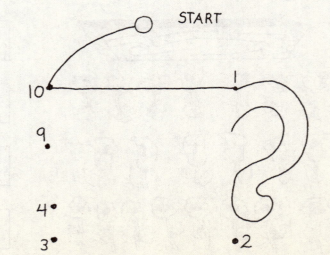

Lesson 1-1 • Numbers 0 Through 10

Name _____ **Lesson 1-2**

We started with __3__ fish.
We bought __2__ more.
How many fish
do we have in all? __5__

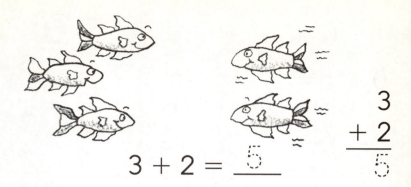

$3 + 2 = \underline{5}$

$$\begin{array}{r} 3 \\ +\,2 \\ \hline 5 \end{array}$$

Add.

1  $\begin{array}{r} 1 \\ +\,2 \\ \hline \end{array}$

2  $\begin{array}{r} 1 \\ +\,1 \\ \hline \end{array}$

3  $\begin{array}{r} 2 \\ +\,1 \\ \hline \end{array}$

4  $\begin{array}{r} 3 \\ +\,0 \\ \hline \end{array}$

5  $\begin{array}{r} 2 \\ +\,2 \\ \hline \end{array}$

6  $\begin{array}{r} 0 \\ +\,2 \\ \hline \end{array}$

7  $\begin{array}{r} 3 \\ +\,1 \\ \hline \end{array}$

8  $\begin{array}{r} 1 \\ +\,4 \\ \hline \end{array}$

Add.

1) 1 + 0 = ___
0 + 1 = ___

2) 2 + 0 = ___
1 + 1 = ___
0 + 2 = ___

3) 3 + 0 = ___
2 + 1 = ___

___ + ___ = 3
___ + ___ = 3

4) 4 + 0 = ___
3 + 1 = ___

___ + ___ = 4
___ + ___ = 4
___ + ___ = 4

5)
___ + ___ = 5
___ + ___ = 5
___ + ___ = 5

___ + ___ = 5
___ + ___ = 5
___ + ___ = 5

6)
```
  2     3     1     2     1     2
 +1    +0    +1    +2    +2    +3
 ___   ___   ___   ___   ___   ___
```

7)
```
  3     1     4     1     3     0
 +2    +3    +1    +4    +1    +4
 ___   ___   ___   ___   ___   ___
```

Name _____   **Lesson 1-3**

Add.

①

0 + 6 = 6   ___ + ___ = 6
1 + 5 = 6   ___ + ___ = 6
___ + ___ = 6   ___ + ___ = 6
___ + ___ = 6   ___ + ___ = 6

② 1 + 1 = ___   4 + 4 = ___   4 + 2 = ___
③ 2 + 2 = ___   5 + 5 = ___   5 + 2 = ___
④ 3 + 3 = ___   3 + 4 = ___   6 + 2 = ___

⑤ 8   0   4   7   1   9   3
  +1   +2   +0   +1   +6   +1   +5

⑥ 2   4   5   3   2   5   6
  +7   +3   +4   +6   +8   +3   +4

Solve.

⑦ Jim saw 4 🐕.   ☐ 4
   Jan saw 5 🐕.   ⊕ ☐ 5
                        _____
   They saw ___ 🐕.   ☐

⑧ Maria picked 5 🌼.   ☐
   Lynn picked 3 🌼.   ◯ ☐
                             _____
   They picked ___ 🌼.   ☐

Lesson 1-3 • Sums Through 10   five **5**

Add.

1.   1   3   4   1   6   3   2
    +9   +6   +2   +2   +1   +7   +2

2.   3   6   4   5   2   5   1
    +2   +2   +1   +2   +6   +1   +8

3.   2   7   2   4   1   8   3
    +1   +2   +8   +6   +7   +2   +1

Complete each table.

4.
Add 3.	
2	5
4	
1	
3	
6	
5	
7	

5.
Add 4.	
1	5
3	
0	
2	
6	
5	
4	

6.
Add 5.	
3	
0	
2	
5	
1	
4	

Name _____

Lesson 1-4

There are _5_ birds in all.
We saw _2_ birds fly away.
How many birds
are left? _3_

5 − 2 = _3_

$$\begin{array}{r} 5 \\ -2 \\ \hline 3 \end{array}$$

Subtract.

1  $\begin{array}{r} 3 \\ -0 \\ \hline \end{array}$ **2**  $\begin{array}{r} 3 \\ -3 \\ \hline \end{array}$

3  $\begin{array}{r} 5 \\ -4 \\ \hline \end{array}$ **4**  $\begin{array}{r} 4 \\ -2 \\ \hline \end{array}$

5   $\begin{array}{r} 3 \\ -1 \\ \hline \end{array}$ **6**  $\begin{array}{r} 5 \\ -3 \\ \hline \end{array}$

7  $\begin{array}{r} 4 \\ -4 \\ \hline \end{array}$ **8**  $\begin{array}{r} 3 \\ -2 \\ \hline \end{array}$

Lesson 1-4 • Subtracting From 5 and Less

Subtract.

1)  5 − 1 = 4

2)  3 − 2

3)  2 − 0

4) 4 − 0

5)  2 − 1

6)  5 − 4

7) 2 − 2

8) 5 − 3

9)  1 − 0

10) 4 − 1

11) 4 − 3

12) 5 − 2

Now Try This!

Write two addition and two subtraction sentences.

2 + 3 = ___   5 − 3 = ___

3 + ___ = ___   5 − ___ = ___

Name _____ Lesson 1-5

Cross out and subtract.

1. 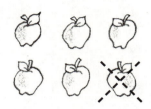 $\begin{array}{r} 6 \\ -1 \\ \hline 5 \end{array}$

2.  $\begin{array}{r} 7 \\ -5 \\ \hline \end{array}$

3. 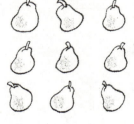 $\begin{array}{r} 9 \\ -3 \\ \hline \end{array}$

4.  $\begin{array}{r} 10 \\ -4 \\ \hline \end{array}$

5. 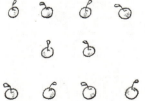 $\begin{array}{r} 10 \\ -6 \\ \hline \end{array}$

6.   $\begin{array}{r} 9 \\ -7 \\ \hline \end{array}$

7.  $\begin{array}{r} 8 \\ -3 \\ \hline \end{array}$

8.  $\begin{array}{r} 10 \\ -3 \\ \hline \end{array}$

Lesson 1-5 • Subtracting From 10 and Less

Subtract.

1. 10 − 3 = ___   8 − 2 = ___   8 − 6 = ___
2. 7 − 4 = ___   6 − 3 = ___   10 − 9 = ___
3. 10 − 5 = ___   9 − 4 = ___   8 − 7 = ___
4. 8 − 5 = ___   10 − 6 = ___   7 − 2 = ___
5. 8 − 4 = ___   10 − 1 = ___   6 − 5 = ___
6. 9 − 5 = ___   9 − 3 = ___   10 − 2 = ___

7.
6	9	7	6	10	9	7
−6	−8	−5	−2	−8	−6	−0

8.
8	6	9	7	10	9	8
−3	−4	−2	−3	−4	−7	−0

Complete each table.

9. Subtract 2.

5	3
7	
8	

10. Subtract 3.

7	4
9	
6	

11. Subtract 5.

8	
6	
10	

Lesson 1-5 • Subtracting From 10 and Less

Lesson 1-6

Name _____

Add.

1. 2   1   5   3   6   1   7
      +2   +1   +2   +2   +1   +4   +2

2. 4   6   2   5   3   4   1
      +1   +3   +6   +1   +7   +2   +9

3. 0   3   8   1   5   2   4
      +4   +3   +1   +6   +0   +1   +5

4. 1   8   4   2   7   6   2
      +2   +0   +3   +8   +1   +4   +5

5. 3   5   1   5   6   8   3
      +4   +3   +8   +5   +2   +2   +1

6. 7   4   2   3   0   1   9
      +3   +4   +3   +5   +7   +3   +1

7. 2   3   1   4   1   5   2
      +4   +6   +5   +6   +7   +4   +7

Lesson 1-6 • Mixed Practice   eleven 11

Subtract.

1.   5 − 1   9 − 3   8 − 6   6 − 5   10 − 3   6 − 2   10 − 1

2.   8 − 2   6 − 3   9 − 8   7 − 6   5 − 5   3 − 1   9 − 4

3.   7 − 3   8 − 5   9 − 1   10 − 5   5 − 2   10 − 2   4 − 3

4.   10 − 7   8 − 4   4 − 0   8 − 3   7 − 7   4 − 1   10 − 9

5.   6 − 4   9 − 6   6 − 1   10 − 6   8 − 7   9 − 5   9 − 7

Now Try This!

Write the missing numbers.   *It's Algebra!*

1.   7 + [3] = 10   4 + [ ] = 8   3 + [ ] = 9

2.   4 − [1] = 3   7 − [ ] = 5   6 − [ ] = 3

Name _____

**Problem Solving
Lesson 1-7**

It's Algebra!

Solve.

1 Mark bought a 🧤 4¢ and a 🦋 3¢. How much did both cost? _7_ ¢

4¢ + 3¢ = _7_ ¢

2 Sam bought a 🚐 5¢ and a 🐰 2¢. How much did both cost? ____ ¢

5¢ + 2¢ = ____ ¢

3 Mary bought a 🐷 8¢ and a 🧸 1¢. How much did both cost? ____ ¢

8¢ + 1¢ = ____ ¢

4 Andy bought a 🚂 3¢ and a ✈️ 7¢. How much did both cost? ____ ¢

3¢ + 7¢ = ____ ¢

5 Ann bought a ✈️ 7¢ and a 🐰 2¢. How much did both cost? ____ ¢

_7_ ¢ ⊕ _2_ ¢ = ____ ¢

6 Meg bought a 🍪 4¢ and a 🏠 4¢. How much did both cost? ____ ¢

____ ¢ ◯ ____ ¢ = ____ ¢

7 Frank bought a 🚗 6¢ and a 🧤 4¢. How much did both cost? ____ ¢

____ ¢ ◯ ____ ¢ = ____ ¢

8 Sue bought a ⛵ 3¢ and a 🚐 5¢. How much did both cost? ____ ¢

____ ¢ ◯ ____ ¢ = ____ ¢

Lesson 1-7 • Problem Solving: Write a Number Sentence

thirteen **13**

Solve.

1 Aaron had 7¢.

He bought a ✏️ (4¢).

How much was left? 3 ¢

7¢ − 4¢ = 3 ¢

2 Dawn had 9¢.

She bought a 🔔 (3¢).

How much was left? ____ ¢

9¢ − 3¢ = ____ ¢

3 Tina had 8¢.

She bought a 🖼️ (5¢).

How much was left? ____ ¢

8¢ − 5¢ = ____ ¢

4 Rex had 9¢.

He bought a 🔑 (4¢).

How much was left? ____ ¢

9¢ − 4¢ = ____ ¢

5 Randy had 8¢.

He bought a 🐭 (7¢).

How much was left? ____ ¢

8 ¢ ⊖ 7 ¢ = ____ ¢

6 Juan had 9¢.

He bought a ⚽ (3¢).

How much was left? ____ ¢

____ ¢ ◯ ____ ¢ = ____ ¢

7 Tom had 10¢.

He bought a 🐰 (4¢).

How much was left? ____ ¢

____ ¢ ◯ ____ ¢ = ____ ¢

8 Tracy had 10¢.

She bought a 🔒 (3¢).

How much was left? ____ ¢

____ ¢ ◯ ____ ¢ = ____ ¢

Lesson 1-7 • Problem Solving: Write a Number Sentence

Name _____   Chapter 1 Test

Match.

1)

2	< three
3	< five
5	< two

Add.

2) 1   3   4   3   2   4   1
   +1   +1   +5   +0   +7   +3   +4

3) 2   5   2   3   3   2   3
   +8   +1   +5   +3   +7   +4   +6

4) 2   5   0   5   3   7   6
   +2   +5   +4   +2   +5   +2   +3

5) 7 + 0 = ___   7 + 3 = ___   5 + 3 = ___

6) 3 + 4 = ___   5 + 4 = ___   0 + 8 = ___

7) 2 + 3 = ___   4 + 4 = ___   8 + 1 = ___

8) 1 + 7 = ___   1 + 9 = ___   4 + 6 = ___

Chapter 1 • Test   fifteen 15

Chapter 1 Test

Subtract.

9.
```
  3      2      4      7      6      8      5
 -1     -0     -2     -4     -3     -6     -3
```

10.
```
  6      9     10      6      9      8     10
 -4     -2     -1     -2     -5     -3     -5
```

11. 10 − 2 = ____   10 − 3 = ____   6 − 6 = ____

12. 8 − 4 = ____   7 − 0 = ____   10 − 6 = ____

Solve.

13. Ruth had 6¢. She bought a . How much was left? ____¢

    ____¢ ◯ ____¢ = ____¢

14. Jill had 6¢. She bought a . How much was left? ____¢

    ____¢ ◯ ____¢ = ____¢

15. Hal bought a and a . How much did both cost? ____¢

    ____¢ ◯ ____¢ = ____¢

16. Rose had 8¢. She bought a . How much is left? ____¢

    ____¢ ◯ ____¢ = ____¢

Basic Facts Through 12

Chapter 2

Lesson 2-1

Add.

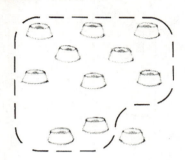

$$\begin{array}{r} 8 \\ +3 \\ \hline 11 \end{array}$$

1)

$$\begin{array}{r} 7 \\ +5 \\ \hline 12 \end{array}$$

2)

$$\begin{array}{r} 5 \\ +6 \\ \hline \end{array}$$

3)

$$\begin{array}{r} 6 \\ +6 \\ \hline \end{array}$$

4)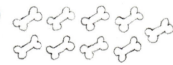

$$\begin{array}{r} 9 \\ +3 \\ \hline \end{array}$$

5)
$$\begin{array}{r} 8 \\ +4 \\ \hline \end{array} \quad \begin{array}{r} 5 \\ +7 \\ \hline \end{array} \quad \begin{array}{r} 4 \\ +4 \\ \hline \end{array} \quad \begin{array}{r} 9 \\ +2 \\ \hline \end{array} \quad \begin{array}{r} 7 \\ +4 \\ \hline \end{array} \quad \begin{array}{r} 9 \\ +3 \\ \hline \end{array} \quad \begin{array}{r} 3 \\ +8 \\ \hline \end{array}$$

6)
$$\begin{array}{r} 4 \\ +7 \\ \hline \end{array} \quad \begin{array}{r} 4 \\ +8 \\ \hline \end{array} \quad \begin{array}{r} 5 \\ +6 \\ \hline \end{array} \quad \begin{array}{r} 3 \\ +9 \\ \hline \end{array} \quad \begin{array}{r} 2 \\ +9 \\ \hline \end{array} \quad \begin{array}{r} 6 \\ +5 \\ \hline \end{array} \quad \begin{array}{r} 7 \\ +5 \\ \hline \end{array}$$

Lesson 2-1 • Sums Through 12

seventeen **17**

Complete each wheel.

Add.

2. 7   9   8   5   4   6   9
   +2   +1   +4   +5   +7   +6   +3

3. 4   6   2   8   3   7   3
   +5   +3   +7   +2   +9   +5   +6

4. 8   5   4   7   3   6   9
   +3   +6   +6   +4   +8   +4   +2

5. 4   6   3   5   7   2   5
   +8   +5   +7   +4   +3   +8   +7

Name _____

Lesson 2-2

Add.

```
   9      7      5      8      6      3      4
 + 1    + 3    + 4    + 2    + 5    + 7    + 8
```

```
   5      8      2      3      7      2      6
 + 7    + 4    + 8    + 6    + 4    + 9    + 4
```

Complete each table.

Add 6.	
2	8
4	
6	
3	
5	

Add 4.	
4	8
5	
7	
8	
6	

Add 3.	
5	
7	
4	
9	
6	

Add 5.	
5	
7	
4	
6	
3	

Solve.

 Ken has 9 shells. He finds 3 more. How many shells does Ken have?

____ shells

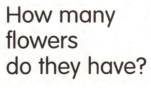 Megan picks 5 flowers. Rich picks 6 flowers. How many flowers do they have?

____ flowers

Lesson 2-2 • Practice Sums Through 12   nineteen **19**

Add.

① 7 + 2   1 + 9   4 + 6   3 + 8   6 + 4   5 + 4   1 + 8

② 6 + 6   8 + 2   7 + 3   3 + 7   5 + 6   9 + 1   4 + 7

③ 1 + 1 = ___   8 + 4 = ___   2 + 8 = ___

④ 2 + 2 = ___   7 + 5 = ___   9 + 3 = ___

⑤ 3 + 3 = ___   6 + 5 = ___   8 + 3 = ___

⑥ 4 + 4 = ___   5 + 7 = ___   9 + 2 = ___

⑦ 5 + 5 = ___   2 + 9 = ___   4 + 8 = ___

Now Try This!

Circle pairs of numbers.   It's Algebra!

① **Sums of 11**

2	6	3	8
9	7	4	4
2	6	2	7
6	5	8	3

(There are 8 pairs.)

② **Sums of 12**

4	8	2	5
9	3	8	7
8	9	6	6
4	7	7	5

(There are 7 pairs.)

Name _____

Problem Solving
Lesson 2-3

These items were found on Pete's desk.

Make a tally mark | for each item. 𝐼𝐼𝐼𝐼 stands for 5 items.

Item	Tally	Number
Pencil	𝐼𝐼𝐼𝐼	5
Eraser		
Crayon		
Marker		

Use the table to answer each question.

① How many erasers are on Pete's desk?

____ erasers

② How many more crayons than markers are on Pete's desk?

____ more crayons

③ Which item does Pete have the most of?

_____

④ Pete also has 6 pens on his desk. How many pens and pencils does he have altogether?

____ pens and pencils

Lesson 2-3 • Problem Solving: Make and Use a Table

twenty-one **21**

Make a table about the fruit in the picture. Then use the table to answer each question.

Pieces of Fruit at a Picnic		
Fruit	Tally	Number
Apples		
Bananas		
Pears		
Watermelon		

1. How many bananas are there?

____ bananas

2. How many more apples are there than pears?

____ more apples

3. Which fruit has the fewest pieces?

_____

4. Which fruit has the most pieces?

_____

5. There are 3 more strawberries than apples. How many strawberries are there?

____ strawberries

6. Lisa counted the apples. Mike counted the bananas. Who counted more pieces of fruit?

_____

Lesson 2-3 • Problem Solving: Make and Use a Table

Name _____

Lesson 2-4

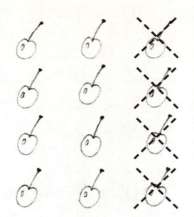

How many cherries are there? 12

How many are crossed out? 4

How many are left? 8

12
− 4
―――
  8

Cross out and subtract.

1  11
− 5
―――

2 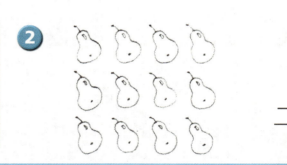 12
− 6
―――

3  12
− 3
―――

4  11
− 2
―――

Subtract.

5
11 11 11 11 12 12 12
− 3 − 8 − 7 − 4 − 3 − 9 − 6

6
11 11 12 12 11 12 12
− 5 − 6 − 5 − 7 − 9 − 4 − 8

Lesson 2-4 • Subtracting From 12 and Less

twenty-three **23**

Subtract.

1. 8 − 1 = ___   11 − 6 = ___   10 − 1 = ___
2. 10 − 2 = ___   9 − 1 = ___   12 − 8 = ___
3. 11 − 4 = ___   12 − 7 = ___   8 − 2 = ___
4. 9 − 0 = ___   10 − 9 = ___   10 − 4 = ___
5. 11 − 5 = ___   8 − 7 = ___   12 − 5 = ___
6. 10 − 3 = ___   12 − 6 = ___   8 − 3 = ___

7. 9   10   9   11   9   11   8
   −2 −8 −9 −3 −4 −8 −6

8. 9   10   8   9   12   10   9
   −8 −5 −4 −3 −4 −6 −7

9. 8   11   9   10   12   8   11
   −8 −7 −6 −7 −3 −5 −9

24 twenty-four   Lesson 2-4 • Subtracting From 12 and Less

Name _____

Lesson 2-5

Subtract.

1)
11	11	11	11	11	11	11
− 3	− 5	− 9	− 4	− 7	− 6	− 8

2)
12	12	12	12	12	12	12
− 3	− 5	− 6	− 8	− 4	− 7	− 9

Complete each wheel.

3) 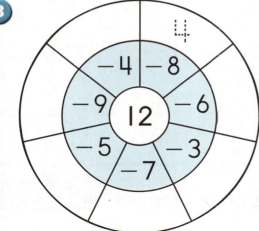  4)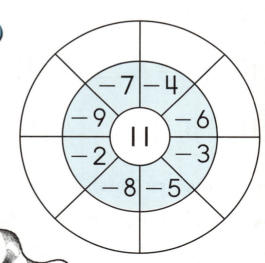

Solve.

5) Janice has 11 .
She read 5 of them.
How many books are left to read?
____ books

6) Jim had 12 .
He ate 7 of them.
How many grapes are left?
____ grapes

Lesson 2-5 • Practice Subtracting From 12 and Less

twenty-five **25**

Subtract.

1. 10 − 3 = ___   8 − 2 = ___   10 − 8 = ___
2. 9 − 1 = ___   11 − 3 = ___   11 − 5 = ___
3. 11 − 4 = ___   10 − 4 = ___   9 − 3 = ___
4. 10 − 7 = ___   12 − 3 = ___   12 − 5 = ___
5. 8 − 7 = ___   10 − 5 = ___   12 − 6 = ___
6. 11 − 2 = ___   12 − 8 = ___   10 − 2 = ___
7. 12 − 4 = ___   10 − 9 = ___   11 − 6 = ___
8. 10 − 1 = ___   11 − 7 = ___   12 − 9 = ___
9. 11 − 8 = ___   12 − 7 = ___   10 − 6 = ___

Now Try This!

Use these numbers to write four number sentences. *It's Algebra!*

| 5   11   6 | | 4   12   8 |

_5_ + _6_ = _11_   _4_ + ___ = _12_
___ + ___ = ___   ___ + ___ = ___
_11_ − _6_ = _5_   ___ − ___ = ___
___ − ___ = ___   ___ − ___ = ___

Lesson 2-5 • Practice Subtracting From 12 and Less

Name _____

Lesson 2-6

Match.

① | 7 + 2 | 5 + 6 | 3 + 5 | ② | 4 + 8 | 5 + 5 | 4 + 3 |

    8   9   11   10   7   12

③ | 12 − 3 | 10 − 5 | 11 − 3 | ④ | 12 − 8 | 11 − 4 | 12 − 6 |

    8   9   5   7   6   4

Add or subtract.

⑤   1   6   0   10   11   3   2
   +5   +5   +7   −2   −2   +9   +7

⑥ 11   10   4   12   12   5   11
   −4   −5   +8   −7   −3   +6   −3

⑦ 12   11   9   3   1   10   12
   −9   −5   +3   +7   +9   −7   −3

⑧ 12   11   2   11   7   5   8
   −5   −8   +9   −6   +4   +7   +4

Add or subtract.

1. 2 + 9 = ___
2. 5 + 7 = ___
3. 8 + 3 = ___
4. 10 − 1 = ___
5. 11 − 4 = ___
6. 12 − 6 = ___
7. 7 + 5 = ___
8. 8 + 2 = ___
9. 4 + 7 = ___
10. 10 − 5 = ___
11. 12 − 9 = ___
12. 6 + 5 = ___

13.
   9   4   11   3
+1   +8   −9   +8

14.
   6   12   11   12
+4   −7   −5   −8

15.
 12   3   9   5
−3   +7   +3   +5

16.
   8   10   12   11
+4   −6   −5   −3

17.
 10   3   11   6
−8   +9   −7   +6

Now Try This!

Write the correct sign.   *It's Algebra!*

1.   8
 ◯ 3
 ――
   5

2.   12
 ◯ 7
 ――
   5

3.   4
 ◯ 5
 ――
   9

4.   6
 ◯ 6
 ――
   0

5.   7
 ◯ 4
 ――
  11

Name _____

Problem Solving
Lesson 2-7

1 nickel — 5 cents 5¢

1 penny — 1 cent 1¢

"Five, six, seven, eight, nine. I have 9 cents."

__9__ ¢

Use the coins to answer each problem.

I have this much.	I saved this much.	How much do I have?
1 __7__ ¢	__4__ ¢	7¢ + 4¢ = 11¢
2 ___ ¢	___ ¢	☐¢ + ☐¢ = ___¢
3 ___ ¢	___ ¢	☐¢ + ☐¢ = ___¢

Lesson 2-7 • Problem Solving: Act It Out

Use the coins to answer each problem.

I have this much.	I spent this much.	How much is left?
1) 11 ¢	5¢	11 ¢ − 5 ¢ = 6 ¢
2) ___ ¢	7¢ ___ ¢	☐ ¢ − ☐ ¢ = ___ ¢
3) ___ ¢	8¢ ___ ¢	☐ ¢ − ☐ ¢ = ___ ¢
4) ___ ¢	7¢ ___ ¢	☐ ¢ − ☐ ¢ = ___ ¢

30 thirty Lesson 2-7 • Problem Solving: Act It Out

Name _____ Chapter 2 Test

Add.

1.
1	8	8	5	3	3	5
+9	+4	+3	+6	+9	+7	+7

2.
6	9	4	2	6	7	3
+5	+3	+8	+9	+6	+4	+8

Subtract.

3.
11	11	10	10	11	11	12
−2	−9	−7	−3	−5	−6	−6

4.
12	12	11	11	12	11	12
−4	−8	−7	−4	−5	−3	−7

Solve.

5. Kay had 11¢. She spent 6¢. How much money does she have left?

____ ¢

6. Dan bought a ruler for 7¢ and an eraser for 5¢. How much money did he spend?

____ ¢

Cumulative Assessment

Add or subtract.

1) $1 + 2 = $ ___ $9 - 3 = $ ___ $1 + 5 = $ ___

2) $7 - 4 = $ ___ $8 - 2 = $ ___ $3 + 3 = $ ___

3) $2 + 4 = $ ___ $6 - 1 = $ ___ $9 + 3 = $ ___

4) $5 + 3 = $ ___ $7 + 5 = $ ___ $6 + 4 = $ ___

5)
```
  9      4      2      5      8      9     10
 -4     +4     +7     +5     -5     -6     -5
```

6)
```
 11     12     10      9      6     11     12
 -3     -5     -2     +1     +3     -6     -8
```

7)
```
  5      8      6      4      3     10     12
 -5     +3     +5     +8     +7     -7     -9
```

Solve.

8) Adam had 4¢ and saved 5¢. How much money did Adam have altogether?

___¢

9) Molly had 11¢. She spent 4¢. How much money did Molly have left?

___¢

Addition Facts Through 18

Chapter 3

Lesson 3-1

Write the numbers.

10 + 1 = 11   10 + 2 = ___   10 + 3 = ___   10 + 4 = ___
eleven   twelve   thirteen   fourteen

10 + 5 = ___   10 + 6 = ___   10 + 7 = ___   10 + 8 = ___
fifteen   sixteen   seventeen   eighteen

Match.

19	fifteen	10 + 5
15	nineteen	10 + 2
12	twelve	10 + 9
11	fourteen	10 + 3
13	eleven	10 + 1
14	thirteen	10 + 4
17	sixteen	10 + 8
16	eighteen	10 + 7
18	seventeen	10 + 6

Lesson 3-1 • Numbers Through 19

thirty-three 33

Write each number.

1. eleven 11
2. eighteen ____
3. fourteen ____
4. twelve ____
5. ten ____
6. seventeen ____
7. nineteen ____
8. thirteen ____
9. sixteen ____
10. fifteen ____
11. zero ____
12. nine ____

Add. Color by answers.

11 red   12 blue   13 green
14 black   15 orange   16 brown
17 yellow   18 purple   19 pink

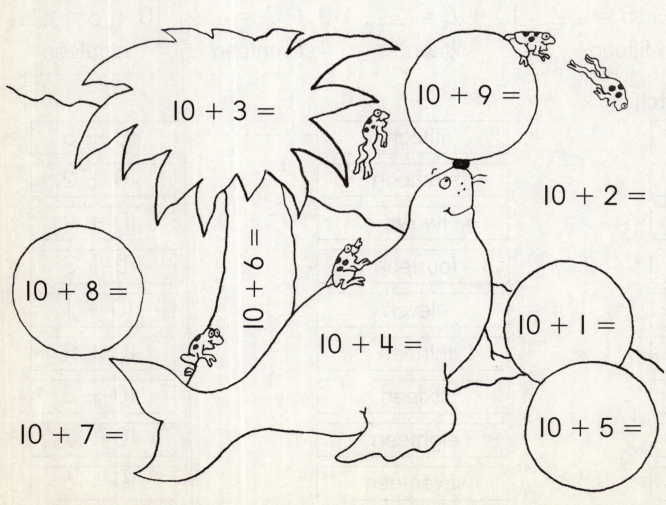

34 thirty-four   Lesson 3-1 • Numbers Through 19

Name _____   Lesson 3-2

      8 + 3 = __11__   8
                                                                    + 3
                                                                    ____
                                                                     11

Add.

1    7
       + 3
                            ____
                             10

2 (stars)   6
               + 6
               ____

3 5   7   1   9   3   5   9
      +5   +4   +9   +2   +8   +7   +1
      ___ ___ ___ ___ ___ ___ ___

4 2   5   7   8   9   6   8
      +8   +6   +3   +2   +3   +5   +4
      ___ ___ ___ ___ ___ ___ ___

5 3   3   4   6   2   7   4
      +7   +9   +8   +4   +9   +5   +7
      ___ ___ ___ ___ ___ ___ ___

Solve.

6 Mitch planted 8 tulips. Then he planted 3 more. How many tulips did Mitch plant?

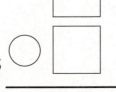

____ tulips

7 Tony saw 6 horses. Karyn saw 6 cows. How many animals did they see?

____ animals

Lesson 3-2 • Review Sums Through 12   thirty-five **35**

Add.

1) 3 + 9   5 + 5   3 + 6   8 + 2   5 + 3   9 + 1   8 + 4

2) 5 + 7   1 + 9   7 + 3   6 + 5   4 + 8   3 + 3   7 + 5

3) 3 + 4   7 + 4   8 + 3   4 + 5   7 + 2   4 + 4   2 + 9

4) 6 + 6   9 + 3   4 + 7   5 + 3   2 + 8   9 + 2   4 + 6

Now Try This!

Write the missing numbers.   *It's Algebra!*

1) 5 + ☐ = 7 (2)   8 + ☐ = 10   6 + ☐ = 12   5 + ☐ = 10   3 + ☐ = 11

2) 8 − ☐ = 3   10 − ☐ = 6   9 − ☐ = 4   11 − ☐ = 6   12 − ☐ = 5

Name _____

Lesson 3-3

Add.

 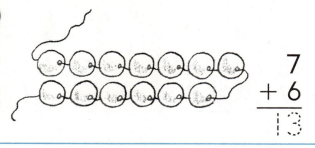
        7
       + 6
        13

        7
       + 7

 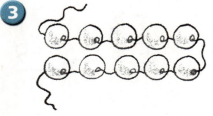
        5
       + 5

 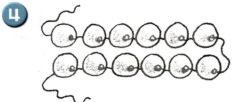
        6
       + 6

        5
       + 8

        9
       + 5

7 8   6   3   8   4   7   9
   +4 +7 +8 +6 +9 +4 +3

8 4   7   5   9   6   9   5
   +8 +5 +9 +2 +8 +4 +6

9 2   8   4   3   8   6   5
   +9 +5 +7 +9 +3 +5 +7

Lesson 3-3 • Sums Through 14   thirty-seven **37**

Add.

1. 5 + 5 = ___
2. 8 + 2 = ___
3. 5 + 6 = ___
4. 3 + 7 = ___
5. 3 + 9 = ___
6. 7 + 4 = ___
7. 4 + 7 = ___
8. 8 + 6 = ___
9. 7 + 5 = ___
10. 4 + 6 = ___
11. 6 + 6 = ___
12. 5 + 9 = ___

13.
  9   3   7   4
+2   +8   +7   +9

14.
  5   6   8   9
+7   +8   +5   +3

15.
  6   6   8   1
+7   +5   +3   +9

16.
  2   9   5   6
+8   +5   +8   +4

17.
  8   2   4   9
+4   +9   +8   +4

Now Try This!

Use these numbers to write addition sentences.

It's Algebra!

1. 8   6   4   2

  6 + 2 = 8

  4 + ___ = ___

2. 9   5   14   4

  ___ + ___ = ___

  ___ + ___ = ___

Name _____   **Lesson 3-4**

  4¢   6¢   8¢   7¢   5¢

Find the total cost.

1   8 ¢ + 6 ¢ = 14 ¢

2   4 ¢ + 8 ¢ = 12 ¢

3   ☐ ¢ + ☐ ¢ = ___ ¢

4   ☐ ¢ + ☐ ¢ = ___ ¢

5   ☐ ¢ + ☐ ¢ = ___ ¢

6   ☐ ¢ + ☐ ¢ = ___ ¢

7   ☐ ¢ + ☐ ¢ = ___ ¢

8   ☐ ¢ + ☐ ¢ = ___ ¢

9   ☐ ¢ + ☐ ¢ = ___ ¢

Fill in the missing word, number, and sign.

10 Dean bought 1 pear. He also bought an _____ . He spent 12¢.

○ ☐ 8¢
  12¢

11 Carla bought 1 orange. She also bought a _____ . She spent 14¢.

○ ☐ 6¢
  14¢

Lesson 3-4 • Money Sums Through 14¢   thirty-nine **39**

Add.

1. 5¢ + 5¢ = __10__ ¢   4¢ + 6¢ = ____   7¢ + 4¢ = ____
2. 2¢ + 8¢ = ____   8¢ + 4¢ = ____   6¢ + 4¢ = ____
3. 5¢ + 4¢ = ____   1¢ + 9¢ = ____   5¢ + 6¢ = ____
4. 4¢ + 7¢ = ____   6¢ + 5¢ = ____   1¢ + 9¢ = ____

5.
6¢	8¢	7¢	7¢	5¢	8¢	4¢
+ 8¢	+ 3¢	+ 5¢	+ 6¢	+ 7¢	+ 5¢	+ 9¢

6.
5¢	9¢	3¢	8¢	9¢	6¢	7¢
+ 9¢	+ 3¢	+ 7¢	+ 6¢	+ 2¢	+ 7¢	+ 3¢

7.
4¢	9¢	3¢	5¢	9¢	7¢	3¢
+ 8¢	+ 4¢	+ 9¢	+ 8¢	+ 5¢	+ 7¢	+ 8¢

Solve.

8. Lauren has 9¢. Becky has 4¢. How much do the girls have altogether?

____ ¢

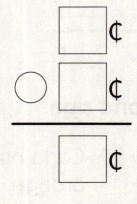

9. Mike bought a ball for 7¢ and a sticker for 7¢. How much did he spend?

____ ¢

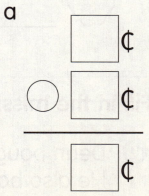

Name _____

Lesson 3-5

Add.

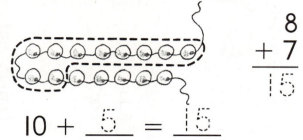

1. 8 + 7 = 15 ; 10 + 5 = 15
2. 8 + 8 ; 10 + 6 = ___

3. 6 + 9
4. 7 + 8
5. 7 + 9

6. 8+5   4+8   7+6   5+9   6+6   7+7   9+4

7. 9+5   5+7   4+9   8+6   3+9   5+8   6+7

Solve.

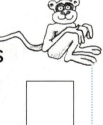
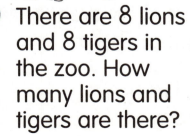

8. There are 7 monkeys in a tree. There are 5 monkeys on the ground. How many monkeys are there altogether?

____ monkeys

9. There are 8 lions and 8 tigers in the zoo. How many lions and tigers are there?

____ lions and tigers

Lesson 3-5 • Sums Through 16

forty-one **41**

Add.

 1. 9   8   7   9   7   5   5
   +2   +3   +5   +3   +7   +9   +5

2. 7   6   8   4   3   8   9
   +4   +6   +5   +7   +9   +8   +5

3. 6   9   4   7   3   7   6
   +5   +4   +8   +6   +8   +4   +9

4. 8 + 6 = ___   7 + 8 = ___   6 + 8 = ___

5. 4 + 9 = ___   6 + 5 = ___   5 + 7 = ___

6. 6 + 7 = ___   8 + 7 = ___   9 + 6 = ___

7. 8 + 4 = ___   5 + 8 = ___   7 + 9 = ___

Solve.

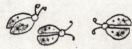

8. There are 9 children playing tag. There are 6 more playing kickball. How many children are playing?

___ children

9. Luis saw 7 ladybugs. Then he saw 9 more. How many ladybugs did Luis see?

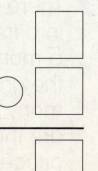

___ ladybugs

42 forty-two   Lesson 3-5 • Sums Through 16

Lesson 3-6

Add.

1. 8 + 9 = 17; 10 + 7 = 17

2. 9 + 9 = __ ; 10 + 8 = __

3. 8 + 8

4. 7 + 9

5. 9 + 8

6. 9+5 7+5 8+5 9+3 4+8 8+8 7+9

7. 7+8 3+9 9+6 6+7 8+4 9+4 6+8

8. 6+6 8+6 5+7 9+8 8+9 7+6 4+9

9. 5+9 8+7 7+7 9+9 5+8 9+7 6+9

Lesson 3-6 • Sums Through 18

Complete each wheel.

1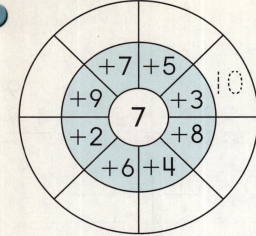

2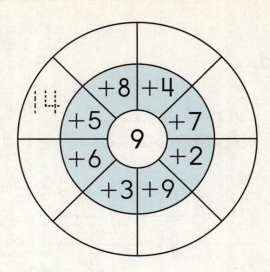

Complete each table.

3

Add 6.	
3	9
7	
4	
9	
2	

4

Add 5.	
3	8
7	
8	
9	
5	

5

Add 8.	
3	11
7	
6	
9	
8	

Solve.

6 Joe saw 7 red roses and 9 yellow roses. How many roses did Joe see?

_____ roses

7 Rita has 8 pennies. Kim has 6 pennies. How many pennies do they have altogether?

_____ pennies

Name _____

Lesson 3-7

It's Algebra!

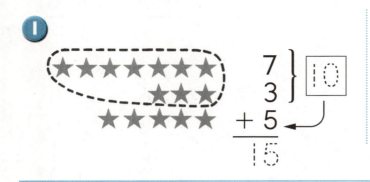

Add. Look for a ten.

1) 7 } 10
    3
   +5

   15

2) 2
    2
    6 }
   +4

3) 5
    4
   +5

4) 8
    2
    4
   +1

5)
9	6	5	1	4	3	2
1	4	5	9	2	7	2
+7	+4	+8	+7	+4	+8	+8

6)
7	8	2	2	2	3	1
3	2	8	6	4	2	5
+6	+7	+6	1	4	4	5
			+4	+8	+8	+5

Lesson 3-7 • Column Addition

forty-five **45**

Add.

1.
```
  2     2     3     3     7     7     1
  3     7     2     7     2     3     1
+ 7   + 3   + 7   + 2   + 3   + 2   + 1
```

2.
```
  2     3     4     5     6     7     8
  2     3     4     5     6     3     2
+ 2   + 3   + 4   + 5   + 4   + 7   + 8
```

3.
```
  4     5     2     3     7     6     4
  2     1     3     6     1     2     4
  3     2     4     1     1     1     1
+ 7   + 6   + 8   + 5   + 6   + 7   + 3
```

Now Try This!

Write two addition number sentences using each number only once.

1. △1 △2 △3 △4 △5 △7

   1 + 3 = 4
   2 + __ = __

2. 2 3 4 5 6 8

   __ + __ = __
   __ + __ = __

Lesson 3-7 • Column Addition

Name _____

Lesson 3-8

1 penny 1¢   1 nickel 5¢

$$\begin{array}{r} 1¢ \\ + 5¢ \\ \hline 6¢ \end{array}$$

Count each amount. Then add.

1)

_5_ ¢   _7_ ¢

$$\begin{array}{r} \boxed{5}¢ \\ + \boxed{7}¢ \\ \hline 12¢ \end{array}$$

2)

___ ¢   ___ ¢

$$\begin{array}{r} \boxed{}¢ \\ + \boxed{}¢ \\ \hline ¢ \end{array}$$

3)

___ ¢   ___ ¢

$$\begin{array}{r} \boxed{}¢ \\ + \boxed{}¢ \\ \hline ¢ \end{array}$$

4)

___ ¢   ___ ¢

$$\begin{array}{r} \boxed{}¢ \\ + \boxed{}¢ \\ \hline ¢ \end{array}$$

Lesson 3-8 • Money Sums Through 18¢

6¢   7¢ 8¢  9¢

Add.

1) 8¢ + 6¢ = 14¢

2) ___¢ + ___¢ = ___¢

3) ___¢ + ___¢ = ___¢

4) ___¢ + ___¢ = ___¢

5) ___¢ + ___¢ = ___¢

6) ___¢ + ___¢ = ___¢

7) ___¢ + ___¢ = ___¢

8) ___¢ + ___¢ = ___¢

9) ___¢ + ___¢ = ___¢

Now Try This!

Cross out the amount that does not belong.

1) 3¢, ~~5¢~~, + 9¢ = 12¢

2) 8¢, 6¢, + 3¢ = 14¢

3) 5¢, 4¢, + 9¢ = 13¢

4) 8¢, 7¢, + 9¢ = 17¢

5) 9¢, 9¢, + 5¢ = 18¢

Lesson 3-8 • Money Sums Through 18¢

Name _____

Problem Solving
Lesson 3-9

Sometimes a problem has extra information.
There are 8 cars in the parking lot.
~~6 of the cars are green.~~
Then 2 more cars drove in.
How many cars are now in the parking lot?
____ cars

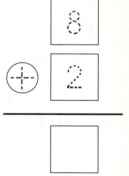

Cross out the extra information. Then solve.

1. Sally found 8 shells.
Trudy found 7 shells.
They put the shells in 2 buckets.
How many shells did they find?
____ shells

2. There were 6 children playing a video game.
3 children wore green shirts.
5 more children joined them.
Now how many children are playing?
____ children

3. 2 children were on line to buy tickets.
Mike used 5 tickets for the roller coaster.
He used 9 tickets for the rocket.
How many tickets did Mike use?
____ tickets

4. 6 children wore red shirts.
9 children wore red shirts.
Mr. Hull wore a green shirt.
How many children wore red shirts?
____ children

Lesson 3-9 • Problem Solving: Too Much Information

forty-nine **49**

Cross out the extra information. Then solve.

1. There are 7 dogs on the grass.
   There are 3 orange cats.
   5 more dogs ran onto the grass.
   How many dogs are on the grass?

   _____ dogs

2. Doug used 5 apples and 8 bananas in a fruit salad.
   He put the fruit in 2 bowls.
   How many pieces of fruit did he use?

   _____ pieces of fruit

3. Lauren ate 9 crackers.
   Chris ate 7 crackers.
   Pedro ate 6 hamburgers.
   How many crackers did they eat?

   _____ crackers

4. Doyle counted 6 green cars.
   He counted 4 blue trucks and 8 red trucks.
   How many trucks did Doyle count?

   _____ trucks

5. Chen built 8 sandcastles.
   Mary dug 3 holes in the sand.
   Leo built 8 sandcastles.
   How many sandcastles did they build?

   _____ sandcastles

6. Larry has 9 keys.
   He has 4 books.
   He gets 8 more keys.
   How many keys does Larry have?

   _____ keys

Lesson 3-9 • Problem Solving: Too Much Information

Name _____

Chapter 3 Test

Add.

①
```
  9      6      7      6      8      6      9
+ 6    + 6    + 4    + 7    + 6    + 5    + 9
```

②
```
  8      2      3      8      7      8      3
+ 3    + 8    + 9    + 8    + 5    + 4    + 7
```

③
```
  8¢     4¢     5¢     7¢     5¢     7¢     9¢
+ 7¢   + 9¢   + 8¢   + 9¢   + 9¢   + 7¢   + 8¢
```

Add.

④
```
  2      5      8      9      7      6      3
  3      4      2      5      3      4      4
+ 4    + 7    + 6    + 1    + 7    + 8    + 7
```

Solve.

⑤ Casey bought one flower for 9¢ and another flower for 7¢. How much did both cost?

_____ ¢

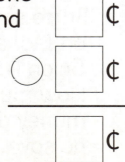

⑥ There were 7 girls and 8 boys at Sandy's party. How many children were at the party?

_____ children

Chapter 3 • Test   fifty-one **51**

Cumulative Assessment

Add or subtract.

1. 12 − 3 = ___   12 − 8 = ___   11 − 2 = ___
2. 11 − 5 = ___   11 − 4 = ___   8 + 4 = ___
3. 5 + 5 = ___   12 − 5 = ___   3 + 8 = ___

Add.

4. 7   8   9   6   7   8   7
   +7   +8   +9   +7   +8   +9   +6

5. 8   9   9   6   8   9   7
   +7   +8   +7   +8   +5   +6   +9

6. 9   5   6   5   5   3   6
                             3   2   4
   +5   +8   +9   +7   +5   +7   +7

Solve.

7. There were 12 frogs. 7 hopped away. How many frogs were left?

   ___ frogs

8. Bruce saved 9¢ on Monday and 5¢ on Friday. How much money did he save?

   ___

   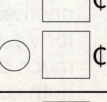

Subtraction Facts Through 18

Chapter 4

Lesson 4-1

How many are there in all? ____
How many are crossed out? ____
How many are left? ____

_12_ – _4_ = ____

Subtract.

1)  $\begin{array}{r} 10 \\ -5 \\ \hline \end{array}$

2)  $\begin{array}{r} 11 \\ -7 \\ \hline \end{array}$

3) $\begin{array}{r} 12 \\ -3 \\ \hline \end{array}$ $\begin{array}{r} 11 \\ -5 \\ \hline \end{array}$ $\begin{array}{r} 10 \\ -1 \\ \hline \end{array}$ $\begin{array}{r} 12 \\ -6 \\ \hline \end{array}$ $\begin{array}{r} 11 \\ -2 \\ \hline \end{array}$ $\begin{array}{r} 10 \\ -5 \\ \hline \end{array}$ $\begin{array}{r} 11 \\ -9 \\ \hline \end{array}$

4) $\begin{array}{r} 10 \\ -2 \\ \hline \end{array}$ $\begin{array}{r} 12 \\ -7 \\ \hline \end{array}$ $\begin{array}{r} 9 \\ -4 \\ \hline \end{array}$ $\begin{array}{r} 10 \\ -6 \\ \hline \end{array}$ $\begin{array}{r} 11 \\ -3 \\ \hline \end{array}$ $\begin{array}{r} 10 \\ -8 \\ \hline \end{array}$ $\begin{array}{r} 12 \\ -9 \\ \hline \end{array}$

5) $\begin{array}{r} 11 \\ -4 \\ \hline \end{array}$ $\begin{array}{r} 9 \\ -1 \\ \hline \end{array}$ $\begin{array}{r} 10 \\ -4 \\ \hline \end{array}$ $\begin{array}{r} 12 \\ -8 \\ \hline \end{array}$ $\begin{array}{r} 11 \\ -8 \\ \hline \end{array}$ $\begin{array}{r} 12 \\ -5 \\ \hline \end{array}$ $\begin{array}{r} 10 \\ -3 \\ \hline \end{array}$

Lesson 4-1 • Review Subtracting From 12 and Less

Complete each table.

1. Subtract 3.

9	6
7	
12	
10	
8	
11	

2. Subtract 4.

11	7
8	
4	
10	
12	
9	

3. Subtract 5.

12	
7	
9	
11	
8	
10	

4. Subtract 6.

7	
9	
6	
10	
8	
11	

Subtract.

5. 8   9   10   11   9   12   11
   −7 −2   −9   −7 −9   −9   −2

6. 10 12   8   9   10   12   11
   −1 −8 −0   −7   −2   −6   −9

7. 9   10 12   11   9   10   7
   −8 −7 −7   −8 −1   −8 −4

Name _____   **Lesson 4-2**

 How many are there in all? ____
How many are crossed out? ____
How many are left? ____

Subtract.

    12
                                        − 5

 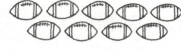   13
                                        − 4

3) 13   13   14   14   11   13   14
   − 4   − 9   − 6   − 8   − 5   − 8   − 7

4) 13   13   12   12   13   14   14
   − 6   − 7   − 5   − 7   − 5   − 5   − 9

Solve.

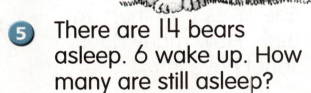

5) There are 14 bears asleep. 6 wake up. How many are still asleep?
   ____ bears

6) There were 13 deer grazing. 5 went to drink water. How many were still grazing?
   ____ deer

Complete each wheel.

1.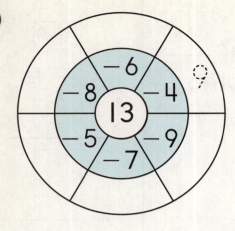

2.

Complete each table.

3. Subtract 3.		4. Subtract 4.		5. Subtract 5.		6. Subtract 6.	
10	7	11	7	10		10	
7		13		12		13	
12		9		11		11	
9		8		14		12	
11		12		13		14	
8		10		9		9	

Solve.

7. Bev puts 13 balls on a shelf. 7 roll off. How many are left on the shelf?
   _____ balls

8. Janet picks 14 flowers. She gives 7 of them to Beth. How many does Janet have left?
   _____ flowers

Name _____

Problem Solving
Lesson 4-3

A line plot is used to organize information. Each X is equal to 1.

This line plot shows how many pets the children in Mr. Jones's class have. How many children have 3 pets?

Number of Pets Children Have

```
                    X
        X    X    X
Number  X    X    X    X
of      X    X    X    X
Children X   X    X    X
        ─┼───┼────┼────┼──▶
         0   1    2    3
           Number of Pets
```

Count the number of Xs to find how many children have 3 pets.

There are __3__ children who have 3 pets.

Use the line plot above to answer each question.

1 How many children do not have pets?

_____ children

2 How many pets do the most children have?

_____ pet

3 Make a tally from the line plot.

Number of Pets	Tally of Students	Number of Students
0	||||	
1		
2		
3		

Lesson 4-3 • Problem Solving: Make and Use a Line Plot   fifty-seven **57**

Miss Johnson asked her class how many brothers they each have. The results are shown in the tally table.

Number of Brothers We Have

Brothers	Tally
0	IIII
1	HHT III
2	HHT
3	II

Use the tally table to complete the line plot.

Number of Brothers We Have

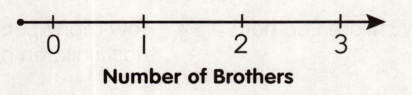

Number of Brothers

1. How many children have 2 brothers?

_____ children

2. How many more children have 1 brother than 3 brothers?

_____ more children

3. How many brothers do the least number of children have?

_____ brothers

4. How many children are in the class altogether?

_____ children

Lesson 4-3 • Problem Solving: Make and Use a Line Plot

Name _____ Lesson 4-4

How many are there in all? ____
How many are crossed out? ____
How many are left? ____

____ − ____ = ____

Subtract.

  15
− 7

 14
− 5

 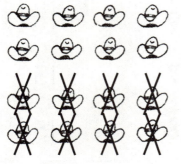 16
− 8

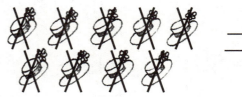 14
− 9

Subtract.

  15   15   13   13   14   14   16
− 6 − 9 − 6 − 7 − 5 − 9 − 8

6. 15   15   14   14   16   16   14
− 8 − 7 − 6 − 8 − 7 − 9 − 7

Lesson 4-4 • Subtracting From 16 and Less   fifty-nine **59**

Subtract to fill in each blank.

 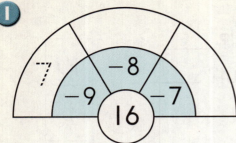 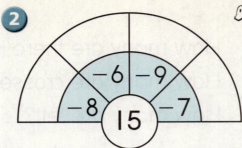

Circle other names for each number.

5) __5__
(12 − 7)
14 − 5
11 − 6
13 − 8

6) __8__
10 − 2
(16 − 8)
14 − 7
13 − 5

7) __4__
14 − 5
13 − 9
11 − 7
12 − 8

8) __7__
14 − 7
16 − 8
13 − 6
15 − 8

9) __9__
14 − 5
16 − 7
13 − 9
11 − 2

10) __6__
12 − 6
14 − 8
13 − 7
15 − 6

11) __3__
12 − 9
9 − 5
10 − 7
11 − 8

12) __8__
16 − 9
14 − 6
15 − 7
13 − 5

Lesson 4-4 • Subtracting From 16 and Less

Name _____   **Lesson 4-5**

How many are there in all? ____
How many flew away? ____
How many are left? ____

Subtract.

①  $\begin{array}{r}18\\-9\\\hline\end{array}$

②  $\begin{array}{r}16\\-8\\\hline\end{array}$

③ $\begin{array}{r}15\\-9\\\hline\end{array}$ $\begin{array}{r}12\\-3\\\hline\end{array}$ $\begin{array}{r}16\\-7\\\hline\end{array}$ $\begin{array}{r}14\\-9\\\hline\end{array}$ $\begin{array}{r}15\\-7\\\hline\end{array}$ $\begin{array}{r}13\\-9\\\hline\end{array}$ $\begin{array}{r}14\\-5\\\hline\end{array}$

④ $\begin{array}{r}12\\-7\\\hline\end{array}$ $\begin{array}{r}17\\-9\\\hline\end{array}$ $\begin{array}{r}15\\-6\\\hline\end{array}$ $\begin{array}{r}14\\-6\\\hline\end{array}$ $\begin{array}{r}12\\-6\\\hline\end{array}$ $\begin{array}{r}17\\-8\\\hline\end{array}$ $\begin{array}{r}13\\-5\\\hline\end{array}$

⑤ $\begin{array}{r}13\\-8\\\hline\end{array}$ $\begin{array}{r}12\\-4\\\hline\end{array}$ $\begin{array}{r}16\\-8\\\hline\end{array}$ $\begin{array}{r}13\\-4\\\hline\end{array}$ $\begin{array}{r}17\\-9\\\hline\end{array}$ $\begin{array}{r}14\\-7\\\hline\end{array}$ $\begin{array}{r}12\\-8\\\hline\end{array}$

⑥ $\begin{array}{r}13\\-6\\\hline\end{array}$ $\begin{array}{r}14\\-8\\\hline\end{array}$ $\begin{array}{r}12\\-5\\\hline\end{array}$ $\begin{array}{r}18\\-9\\\hline\end{array}$ $\begin{array}{r}13\\-7\\\hline\end{array}$ $\begin{array}{r}12\\-9\\\hline\end{array}$ $\begin{array}{r}15\\-8\\\hline\end{array}$

Subtract.

1. 15−9   12−5   14−6   9−9   15−6   12−9   13−5

2. 12−4   17−8   14−9   15−8   12−6   16−9   12−8

3. 10−6   13−8   17−9   12−3   14−7   12−7   16−7

4. 16−8   14−5   15−7   18−9   13−7   14−8   13−6

Now Try This!

Answer each riddle. *It's Algebra!*

1. When you add me to 5, the sum is 11. Who am I? ____

2. When you double me, the sum is 16. Who am I? ____

3. When you add me to 8, the sum is 17. Who am I? ____

4. When you double me and add 1, you get 13. Who am I? ____

Name _____   **Lesson 4-6**

Subtract.

1.
   - 14 − 5
   - 13 − 8
   - 15 − 6
   - 12 − 3
   - 11 − 5
   - 12 − 7
   - 13 − 9

2.
   - 12 − 4
   - 11 − 6
   - 16 − 8
   - 11 − 2
   - 10 − 7
   - 12 − 5
   - 14 − 7

3.
   - 13 − 4
   - 10 − 1
   - 11 − 7
   - 13 − 5
   - 10 − 8
   - 11 − 3
   - 16 − 7

4.
   - 17 − 8
   - 12 − 6
   - 11 − 4
   - 15 − 9
   - 10 − 2
   - 13 − 6
   - 14 − 8

Complete each table.

 Subtract 9.

11	2
15	
18	
13	
17	
14	
16	

 Subtract 8.

11	
15	
17	
14	
12	
16	
13	

 Subtract 7.

13	
10	
15	
12	
16	
14	
11	

 Subtract 6.

9	
14	
11	
12	
13	
10	
15	

Lesson 4-6 • Practice Subtracting From 18 and Less

Subtract.

1. 11 − 8 = ___   16 − 9 = ___   10 − 6 = ___
2. 10 − 3 = ___   10 − 5 = ___   15 − 8 = ___
3. 14 − 6 = ___   12 − 8 = ___   9 − 9 = ___
4. 18 − 9 = ___   10 − 9 = ___   8 − 5 = ___
5. 10 − 4 = ___   13 − 7 = ___   14 − 9 = ___
6. 12 − 9 = ___   9 − 3 = ___   9 − 0 = ___
7. 15 − 7 = ___   17 − 9 = ___   11 − 9 = ___

Complete each wheel.

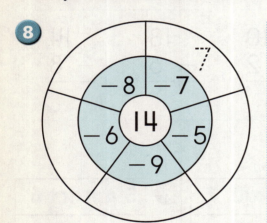
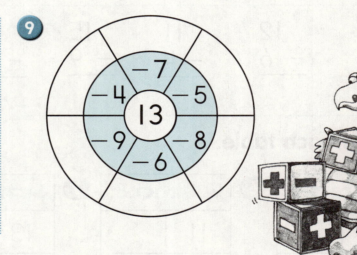

Now Try This!

Write in the correct sign.   *It's Algebra!*

1. 13 ⊖ 6 = 7   16 ◯ 8 = 8   8 ◯ 5 = 13
2. 9 ⊕ 9 = 18   13 ◯ 7 = 6   11 ◯ 5 = 6
3. 8 ◯ 8 = 16   5 ◯ 9 = 14   12 ◯ 6 = 6
4. 17 ◯ 9 = 8   7 ◯ 2 = 9   14 ◯ 5 = 9

Name _____ **Lesson 4-7**

Solve.

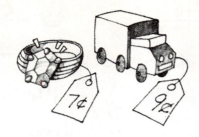 

1 Carlos had 15¢.
He bought a bear.
How much money
is left?

___9___ ¢

2 A truck costs ___9___ ¢.
A ring costs ___7___ ¢.
How much more does
the truck cost?

___2___ ¢

3 Joan had 17¢.
She bought a truck.
How much money
is left?

_____

4 Donna had 15¢.
She bought a train.
How much money
does she have left?

_____

5 Chuck gave the clerk
10¢ to pay for a ring.
How much change did
he get?

_____

6 Marge gave the clerk
10¢ to pay for a car.
How much change did
she get?

_____

7 Dorothy had 18¢.
She bought a truck.
How much does she
have left?

_____

8 Cal had 13¢. He bought a
bear. How much does he
have left?

_____

Lesson 4-7 • Subtracting From 18¢ and Less

Circle other names for each amount.

	① 7¢	② 5¢	③ 4¢	④ 6¢
	(16¢ − 9¢)	12¢ − 7¢	11¢ − 7¢	11¢ − 6¢
	12¢ − 5¢	13¢ − 6¢	13¢ − 9¢	14¢ − 8¢
	13¢ − 8¢	(14¢ − 9¢)	10¢ − 6¢	13¢ − 7¢
	10¢ − 3¢	10¢ − 5¢	12¢ − 7¢	12¢ − 6¢

Subtract.

⑤ 16¢ − 8¢   15¢ − 6¢   14¢ − 7¢   13¢ − 4¢   15¢ − 7¢   17¢ − 9¢

⑥ 14¢ − 5¢   17¢ − 8¢   13¢ − 5¢   15¢ − 8¢   12¢ − 3¢   14¢ − 6¢

⑦ 16¢ − 7¢   12¢ − 4¢   11¢ − 5¢   18¢ − 9¢   12¢ − 8¢   15¢ − 9¢

Now Try This!

①

How much more do two marbles cost than one ball?

_____

② Linda wants to buy a fish for 15¢. She has 8¢. How much more money does she need?

_____

Lesson 4-7 • Subtracting From 18¢ and Less

Name _____

Chapter 4 Test

Subtract.

1.
 | 10 | 13 | 12 | 15 | 8 | 13 | 14 |
 | −7 | −5 | −3 | −6 | −0 | −4 | −7 |

2.
 | 14 | 11 | 13 | 16 | 15 | 13 | 15 |
 | −6 | −5 | −7 | −8 | −9 | −8 | −7 |

3.
 | 17 | 13 | 9 | 16 | 14 | 11 | 12 |
 | −8 | −9 | −9 | −7 | −8 | −4 | −7 |

4.
 | 18 | 14 | 16 | 15 | 13 | 14 | 17 |
 | −9 | −5 | −9 | −8 | −6 | −9 | −9 |

Solve.

5. Brenda saw 14 lightning bugs. Elmer saw 9. How many more lightning bugs did Brenda see?

  _____ lightning bugs

6. Matt has 17 marbles. Paul has 9 marbles. How many more marbles does Matt have?

  _____ marbles

7. Sonja had 15¢. She bought a balloon for 8¢. How much money does she have left?

  _____

8. Roy counted 16 crows. 8 of them flew away. How many are left?

  _____ crows

Cumulative Assessment

Add or subtract.

1.
   - 7 + 0
   - 9 + 1
   - 6 − 5
   - 7 − 5
   - 4 − 0
   - 8 + 2
   - 9 + 7

2.
   - 9 − 3
   - 10 − 5
   - 8 − 7
   - 10 − 9
   - 7 + 3
   - 9 + 5
   - 7 + 6

3.
   - 11 − 4
   - 12 − 7
   - 8 + 4
   - 9 + 3
   - 8 + 8
   - 13 − 5
   - 14 − 7

4.
   - 15 − 6
   - 7 + 9
   - 8 + 6
   - 9 + 9
   - 16 − 7
   - 17 − 9
   - 15 − 8

Solve.

5. Nancy counted 9 deer and 5 wild turkeys. How many animals did she count?

   ____ animals

6. Bert picked 11 tulips. Fay picked 8 tulips. How many more tulips did Bert pick?

   ____ tulips

7. Bill ran 7 blocks. Then he ran 6 blocks more. How many blocks did Bill run?

   ____ blocks

8. There are 12 dogs in the park. 7 dogs run home. How many dogs are left in the park?

   ____ dogs

Name _____

Numbers Through Hundreds

Chapter 5

Lesson 5-1

Write each number.

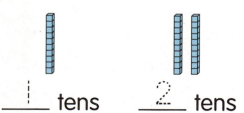

__1__ tens   __2__ tens   ___ tens   ___ tens   ___ tens
ten __10__   twenty __20__   thirty ___   forty ___   fifty ___

___ tens   ___ tens   ___ tens   ___ tens
sixty ___   seventy ___   eighty ___   ninety ___

___ tens   one hundred _____

Write each number.

1   __33__

2   ___

3 ___

4 ___

Write the missing numbers before and after.

5 __15__, 16, __17__

6 ___, 54, ___

7 ___, 31, ___

8 ___, 99, ___

Lesson 5-1 • Numbers Through 100   sixty-nine **69**

Write the missing numbers.

1. 24, 25, 26, _27_, ___, ___, ___, ___, _32_
2. 37, 38, ___, ___, ___, ___, ___, _44_
3. 56, 57, ___, ___, ___, ___, ___, ___
4. 41, 42, ___, ___, ___, ___, ___, ___

Write each number.

5. seventeen _17_
6. fifty-two ___
7. fifteen ___
8. sixty-three ___
9. twelve ___
10. seventy-seven ___
11. fourteen ___
12. eighty-one ___
13. sixteen ___
14. ninety-four ___
15. eighteen ___
16. thirty-five ___
17. twenty-nine ___
18. forty-eight ___

(Now Try This!)

Use these digits to write 2-digit numbers.

1. | 2 | 7 | 6 | _27_, _26_, _72_, _76_, ___, ___
2. | 9 | 1 | 5 | ___, ___, ___, ___, ___, ___

70 seventy

Lesson 5-1 • Numbers Through 100

Name _____

Lesson 5-2

How many hundreds, tens, and ones are there? Write each number.

 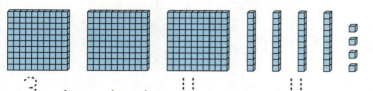

_3_ hundreds _4_ tens _4_ ones _344_

 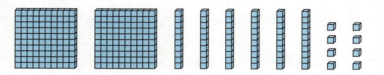

___ hundreds ___ tens ___ ones ___

___ hundreds ___ tens ___ ones ___

___ hundreds ___ tens ___ ones ___

 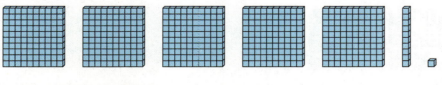

___ hundreds ___ ten ___ one ___

Lesson 5-2 • Counting Hundreds, Tens, and Ones

**How many hunderds, tens, and ones are there?
Write each number.**

1)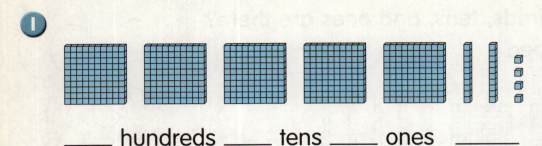

___ hundreds ___ tens ___ ones _____

2)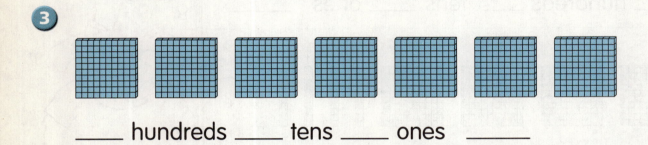

___ hundreds ___ tens ___ ones _____

3)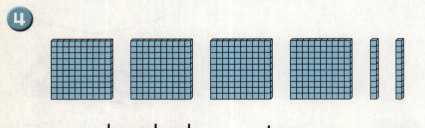

___ hundreds ___ tens ___ ones _____

4)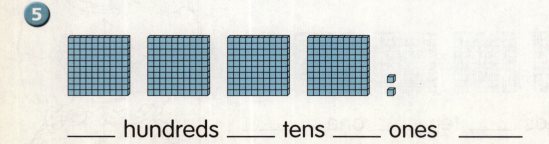

___ hundreds ___ tens ___ ones _____

5)

___ hundreds ___ tens ___ ones _____

Name _____

Lesson 5-3

hundreds tens ones

How many hundreds, tens, and ones are there?
Write each number.

1.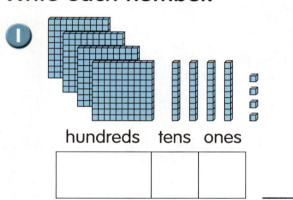

hundreds tens ones

2.

hundreds tens ones

3.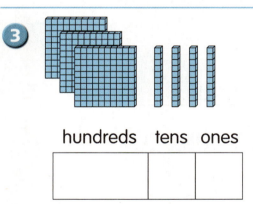

hundreds tens ones

4.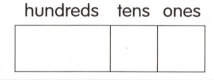

hundreds tens ones

5.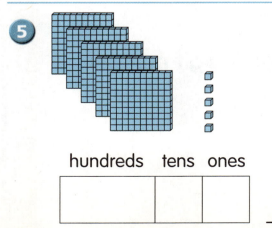

hundreds tens ones

6.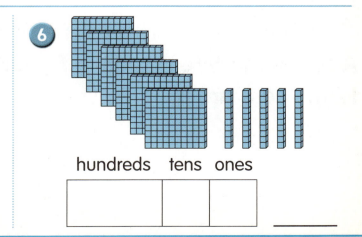

hundreds tens ones

Lesson 5-3 • Place Value Through Hundreds

seventy-three **73**

How many hundreds, tens, and ones are there?
Write each number.

1.

hundreds	tens	ones

   ___

2.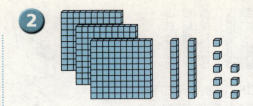

hundreds	tens	ones

   ___

3.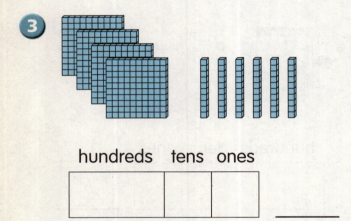

hundreds	tens	ones

   ___

4.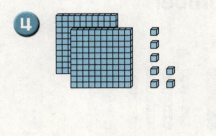

hundreds	tens	ones

   ___

Write each missing number before and after.

5. 614, 615, 616

6. ___, 834, ___

7. ___, 499, ___

8. ___, 200, ___

9. ___, 999, ___

10. ___, 99, ___

(Now Try This!)

Arrange the three cards to form different 3-digit numbers.
Hint: There are 6.

132 ___ ___ ___ ___ ___

Name _____   Lesson 5-4

  130 ¢ $ 1 . 30

Write the amount in two ways.

dollars	cents
2	20

220 ¢ $ 2 . 20

dollars	cents

_____ ¢ $ _____ . _____

dollars	cents

_____ ¢ $ _____ . _____

dollars	cents

_____ ¢ $ _____ . _____

Lesson 5-4 • Counting Dollars, Dimes, and Pennies

Write the amount in two ways.

1.  42 ¢
   $ 0 . 42

2.  ____ ____

3.  ____ ____

4.  ____ ____

5.  ____ ____

6.  ____ ____

7.  ____ ____

8.  ____ ____

9.  ____ ____

10.  ____ ____

Lesson 5-4 • Counting Dollars, Dimes, and Pennies

Name _____ **Lesson 5-5**

Count by ones. Write each missing number.

1) 185, 186, 187, __188__, __189__, ____, ____, ____

2) 96, 97, 98, ____, ____, ____, ____, ____

3) 396, 397, 398, ____, ____, ____, ____, ____

4) 105, 106, ____, ____, ____, ____, ____

5) 215, 216, 217, ____, ____, ____, ____, ____

Count by fives. Write each missing number.

6) 5, 10, 15, ____, ____, ____, ____, ____

7) 105, 110, 115, ____, ____, ____, ____, ____

8) 535, 540, 545, ____, ____, ____, ____, ____

9) 380, 385, 390, ____, ____, ____, ____, ____

Count by tens. Write each missing number.

10) 10, 20, 30, ____, ____, ____, ____, ____

11) 110, 120, 130, ____, ____, ____, ____, ____

12) 450, 460, 470, ____, ____, ____, ____, ____

13) 580, 590, ____, ____, ____, ____, ____, ____

Count by hundreds. Write each missing number.

14) 100, 200, __300__, __400__, ____, ____, ____, ____, ____

Lesson 5-5 • Counting Through 1,000   seventy-seven **77**

What does the blue digit mean? Circle the correct word.

1) 275 — (tens), ones, hundreds

2) 341 — hundreds, tens, ones

3) 204 — ones, tens, hundreds

4) 526 — tens, hundreds, ones

5) 973 — hundreds, ones, tens

6) 858 — tens, ones, hundreds

Write the number of hundreds, tens, and ones.

7) 732 — _2_ ones, _3_ tens, _7_ hundreds

8) 467 — ___ ones, ___ tens, ___ hundreds

9) 618 — ___ ones, ___ ten, ___ hundreds

10) 279 — ___ ones, ___ tens, ___ hundreds

11) 312 — ___ ones, ___ ten, ___ hundreds

12) 103 — ___ ones, ___ tens, ___ hundred

Now Try This!

Solve.

1) I am thinking of a number. It has 2 tens, 3 hundreds, and 5 ones. What is my number?

_____

2) My number has no ones, two hundreds, and no tens. What is my number?

_____

Name _____

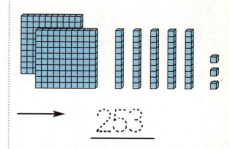

Lesson 5-6

233 ← 10 less   243   10 more → 253

Write each missing number.

	10 less	10 more		10 less	10 more
1	324, 334, 344		9	____, 771, ____
2	____, 80, ____		10	____, 105, ____
3	____, 262, ____		11	____, 593, ____
4	____, 428, ____		12	____, 322, ____
5	____, 110, ____		13	____, 607, ____
6	____, 549, ____		14	____, 989, ____
7	____, 852, ____		15	____, 400, ____
8	____, 901, ____		16	____, 990, ____

Solve.

17 Diane saves baseball cards. She has 210 cards. Her brother has 10 more cards than Diane. How many cards does Diane's brother have?

_____ cards

18 Cynthia has 102 shells in her collection. Dino has 10 fewer shells than Cynthia. How many shells does Dino have?

_____ shells

Lesson 5-6 • 10 More, 10 Less; 100 More, 100 Less   seventy-nine **79**

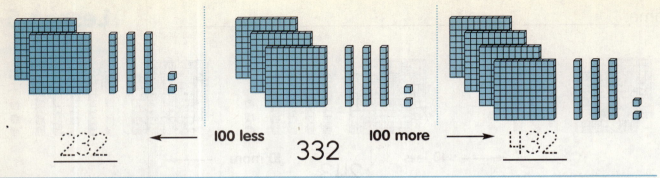

232 ← 100 less 332 100 more → 432

Write the missing numbers.

	100 less	100 more		100 less	100 more
1	235 , 335, 435		8	____, 771, ____	
2	____, 262, ____		9	____, 105, ____	
3	____, 428, ____		10	____, 593, ____	
4	____, 110, ____		11	____, 322, ____	
5	____, 549, ____		12	____, 607, ____	
6	____, 650, ____		13	____, 400, ____	
7	____, 801, ____		14	____, 890, ____	

Solve.

15. The Perez family took a trip. They drove 183 miles on Thursday. On Friday, they drove 100 miles farther than they did on Thursday. How many miles did they drive on Friday?

    ____ miles

16. In a contest, the champion jumped rope 315 times without missing. Marcie jumped 100 times less than the champion. How many times did Marcie jump?

    ____ times

80 eighty

Lesson 5-6 • 10 More, 10 Less; 100 More, 100 Less

Name _____   **Lesson 5-7**

It's Algebra!

 "22 is the same as 22. They are equal."

 "33 has more tens."

"28 and 25 have the same number of tens, but 28 has more ones."

 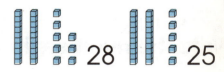

22 is equal to 22.   26 is less than 33.   28 is greater than 25.
22 ◯ 22   26 ◯ 33   28 ⟩ 25

                            33 is greater than 26.   25 is less than 28.
                            33 ◯ 26   25 ⟨ 28

Circle the greater number. Then write >, <, or = in each ◯.

① (87)   83   ② 97   92   ③ 55   59
   87 ◯ 83   97 ◯ 92   55 ◯ 59

④ 48   45   ⑤ 23   23   ⑥ 73   75
   48 ◯ 45   23 ◯ 23   73 ◯ 75

⑦ 64   75   ⑧ 35   25   ⑨ 61   50
   64 ◯ 75   35 ◯ 25   61 ◯ 50

Lesson 5-7 • Comparing 2-Digit Numbers   eighty-one **81**

Write >, <, or = in each ◯.

1. 39 < 93
2. 91 ◯ 97
3. 70 ◯ 60
4. 27 ◯ 38
5. 57 ◯ 67
6. 82 ◯ 72
7. 41 ◯ 41
8. 32 ◯ 52
9. 63 ◯ 63
10. 54 ◯ 65
11. 96 ◯ 89
12. 75 ◯ 57
13. 70 ◯ 50
14. 71 ◯ 71
15. 88 ◯ 98

Write the numbers in order from least to greatest.

16. 39, 29, 61
    ___ ___ ___
    least   greatest

17. 60, 80, 40
    ___ ___ ___
    least   greatest

18. 85, 55, 75
    ___ ___ ___
    least   greatest

19. 51, 34, 19
    ___ ___ ___
    least   greatest

20. 67, 50, 76
    ___ ___ ___
    least   greatest

21. 39, 45, 72
    ___ ___ ___
    least   greatest

Solve.

22. Frank has 38 flower seeds. René has 42 flower seeds. Who has more seeds?

    _____

23. Mei Ling scored 51 points. Richard scored 49 points. Who lost the game?

    _____

Lesson 5-7 • Comparing 2-Digit Numbers

Name _____   **Lesson 5-8**

It's Algebra!

123

123 is greater than 86.
123 > 86

86 is less than 123.
86 < 123

86

123 has more hundreds.

325

325 is less than 349.
325 (<) 349

349

349 is greater than 325.
349 (>) 325

349 and 325 have the same number of hundreds, but 349 has more tens.

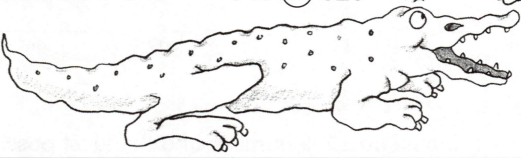

Circle the greater number. Then write >, <, or = in each ◯.

① 67   (167)
   67 (<) 167

② 135   98
   135 ◯ 98

③ 150   150
   150 ◯ 150

④ 246   346
   246 ◯ 346

⑤ 415   396
   415 ◯ 396

⑥ 231   132
   231 ◯ 132

Lesson 5-8 • Comparing 3-Digit Numbers   eighty-three **83**

Write >, <, or = in each ◯.

1. 458 > 302
2. 86 ◯ 129
3. 265 ◯ 265
4. 912 ◯ 832
5. 901 ◯ 109
6. 302 ◯ 298
7. 600 ◯ 706
8. 97 ◯ 79
9. 989 ◯ 999
10. 350 ◯ 450
11. 120 ◯ 120
12. 325 ◯ 523
13. 367 ◯ 367
14. 554 ◯ 455
15. 717 ◯ 698
16. 302 ◯ 285
17. 998 ◯ 998
18. 502 ◯ 499
19. 230 ◯ 99
20. 707 ◯ 706
21. 445 ◯ 435

Write the numbers in order from least to greatest.

22. 301 | 95 | 102
____ ____ ____
least   greatest

23. 249 | 234 | 251
____ ____ ____
least   greatest

24. 9 | 999 | 99
____ ____ ____
least   greatest

25. 275 | 546 | 489
____ ____ ____
least   greatest

Now Try This!

Make the greatest possible number and the least possible number. Use all three number cards each time.

1. 6 | 3 | 9
greatest ____
least ____

2. 2 | 1 | 7
greatest ____
least ____

84 eighty-four   Lesson 5-8 • Comparing 3-Digit Numbers

Name _____   **Lesson 5-9**

First   Second   Third   Fourth   Fifth

The walrus is first. The mouse is fourth.

**Look at Mrs. Jones's class roll.
Tell where each person is in order.**

#	Name	#	Name				
1	Adam	17	Leah	first	Adam	seventeenth	_____
2	Beverly	18	Linda	fourth	_____	nineteenth	_____
3	Bill	19	Mary	eighth	_____	twenty-second	_____
4	Chan	20	Me Lin	twelfth	_____	twenty-sixth	_____
5	Cheryl	21	Mike	sixteenth	_____	thirty-first	_____
6	Diane	22	Noah	fourteenth	_____	twenty-fourth	_____
7	Dick	23	Opal	tenth	_____	eighteenth	_____
8	Dorothy	24	Paul	sixth	_____	thirtieth	_____
9	Emma	25	Raul	second	_____	thirty-second	_____
10	George	26	Rosa	seventh	_____	twenty-fifth	_____
11	Harry	27	Sarah	third	_____	twenty-seventh	_____
12	Isaac	28	Stacey	fifteenth	_____	twenty-ninth	_____
13	Jack	29	Terry	fifth	_____	twentieth	_____
14	Jean	30	Tom	thirteenth	_____	twenty-third	_____
15	Juan	31	Vera	eleventh	_____	twenty-first	_____
16	Ken	32	Wade	ninth	_____	twenty-eighth	_____

Lesson 5-9 • Ordinal Numbers

Sunday	Monday	Tuesday	Wednesday	Thursday	Friday	Saturday
		1	2	3	4	5
6	7	8	9	10	11	12
13	14	15	16	17	18	19
20	21	22	23	24	25	26
27	28	29	30	31		

January

Use the calendar to write the day of the month.

1. first Monday 7
2. fourth Saturday ____
3. second Sunday ____
4. fifth Tuesday ____
5. third Wednesday ____
6. second Friday ____

Use the calendar to write the day of the week.

7. January first Tuesday
8. January sixteenth ____
9. January tenth ____
10. January twelfth ____
11. January eleventh ____
12. January fifteenth ____
13. January thirteenth ____
14. January twenty-first ____
15. January eighteenth ____
16. January seventh ____
17. January thirty-first ____
18. January twenty-sixth ____
19. January thirtieth ____
20. January twentieth ____
21. January seventeenth ____
22. January twenty-eighth ____

Lesson 5-9 • Ordinal Numbers

Name _____

Lesson 5-10

Match the number name to the number.

1. two hundred — 400
2. six hundred — 900
3. nine hundred — 200
4. four hundred — 700
5. seven hundred — 600

6. three hundred seventy — 130
7. one hundred thirty — 490
8. five hundred ten — 860
9. eight hundred sixty — 370
10. four hundred ninety — 510

11. two hundred fifty-three — 255
12. five hundred sixty-six — 998
13. nine hundred ninety-eight — 566
14. five hundred sixteen — 516
15. two hundred fifty-five — 253

16. eight hundred seventy-two — 344
17. three hundred forty-four — 872
18. eight hundred twenty-seven — 418
19. three hundred four — 827
20. four hundred eighteen — 304

Lesson 5-10 • Number Names

eighty-seven **87**

Write each number.

1. forty-five _____
2. nine hundred ninety _____
3. one hundred forty-five _____
4. four hundred five _____
5. two hundred nineteen _____
6. seven hundred eighteen _____
7. five hundred _____
8. ninety-nine _____
9. three hundred ten _____
10. eight hundred eight _____
11. six hundred fifty _____
12. five hundred twenty _____

Solve.

13. I am a number greater than 8 tens and 5 ones. I am less than 8 tens and 7 ones.

    Who am I? _____

14. We are two numbers. We are both less than 8 tens. We are both greater than 77.

    Who are we? _____ _____

15. We are two numbers. We are both less than 2 hundreds and 5 tens, and 6 ones. We are both greater than 2 hundreds 5 tens, 3 ones.

    Who are we? _____, _____

16. I am a 3-digit number. All my digits are the number 3.

    Who am I? _____

17. I am a number 1 less than 1,000.

    Who am I? _____

18. I am a number 100 more than 900.

    Who am I? _____

Problem Solving
Lesson 5-11

You can use a hundred chart to count forward by 10.
You can also use it to count backward by 10.

1	2	3	4	5	6	7	8	9	10
11	12	13	14	15	16	17	18	19	20
21	22	23	24	25	26	27	28	29	30
31	32	33	34	35	36	37	38	39	40
41	42	43	44	45	46	47	48	49	50
51	52	53	54	55	56	57	58	59	60
61	62	63	64	65	66	67	68	69	70
71	72	73	74	75	76	77	78	79	80
81	82	83	84	85	86	87	88	89	90
91	92	93	94	95	96	97	98	99	100

Count forward by tens.

1. 10, 20, ____, 40, 50, ____, 70, 80, ____, 100

2. 5, 15, 25, 35, ____, 55, 65, ____, 85, 95

Count backward by tens.

3. 100, ____, 80, 70, 60, ____, 40, 30, ____, 10

4. 98, 88, ____, 68, ____, 48, 38, ____, 18, 8

Lesson 5-11 • Problem Solving: Look for a Pattern   eighty-nine **89**

Use the hundred chart. Write each number.

1	2	3	4	5	6	7	8	9	10
11	12	13	14	15	16	17	18	19	20
21	22	23	24	25	26	27	28	29	30
31	32	33	34	35	36	37	38	39	40
41	42	43	44	45	46	47	48	49	50
51	52	53	54	55	56	57	58	59	60
61	62	63	64	65	66	67	68	69	70
71	72	73	74	75	76	77	78	79	80
81	82	83	84	85	86	87	88	89	90
91	92	93	94	95	96	97	98	99	100

1. What number is between 74 and 76? _____

2. What number is 10 less than 63? _____

3. What number comes after 47? _____

4. What number is 20 more than 32? _____

5. What number is 30 less than 88? _____

6. What number comes before 40? _____

7. What number is 60 more than 13? _____

8. Name the numbers between 15 and 24. _____

Name _____

Chapter 5 Test

How many hundreds, tens, and ones are there?
Write the number.

     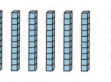

____ hundreds ____ tens ____ ones _____

Write the amount in two ways.

_____

____ . ____

Write each missing number.

③ 125, 126, 127, ____, ____, ____, ____

④ 70, 80, 90, ____, ____, ____, ____

Write the number of hundreds, tens, and ones.

⑤ 971

____ hundreds ____ tens
____ one

⑥ 804

____ hundreds ____ tens
____ ones

Write each missing number before and after.

⑦ ____, 998, ____

⑧ ____, 400, ____

Write >, <, or = in each ◯.

⑨ 342 ◯ 415

⑩ 625 ◯ 625

⑪ 773 ◯ 737

⑫ 899 ◯ 900

Cumulative Assessment

Add or subtract.

1)
$2 + 7$ $5 + 5$ $8 + 3$ $3 + 6$ $11 - 7$ $14 - 6$ $15 - 8$

2)
$12 - 5$ $17 - 8$ $2 + 9$ $9 + 7$ $8 + 8$ $11 - 5$ $15 - 6$

3)
$11 - 8$ $13 - 7$ $10 - 6$ $7 + 7$ $9 + 3$ $8 + 5$ $16 - 7$

4)
$18 - 9$ $14 - 8$ $16 - 9$ $2 + 8$ $7 + 7$ $9 + 9$ $5 + 7$

Solve.

5)

How much do both toys cost altogether?

15¢

6)

How much more does the truck cost?

9¢

92 ninety-two — Chapter 5 • Cumulative Assessment

Name _____

Time and Money

Chapter 6

Lesson 6-1

There are 12 hour marks on a clock. Write the hour numbers on the clock.

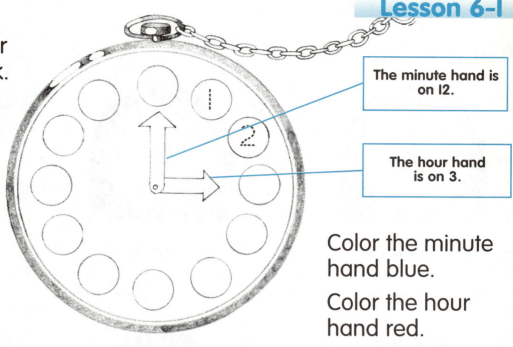

The minute hand is on 12.

The hour hand is on 3.

It is 3 o'clock. We can also write 3:00.

Color the minute hand blue.

Color the hour hand red.

Match the clocks that show the same time.

1.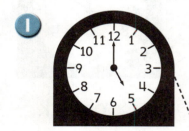

2.

3.

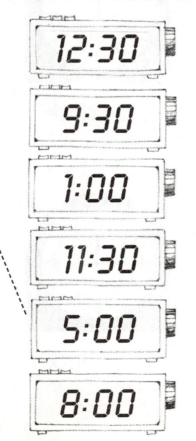

4.

5.

6.

Lesson 6-1 • Telling Time to the Hour and Half-Hour

ninety-three **93**

　　seven thirty
　　7:30

Write each time.

1

_5_ o'clock

_5_ : _00_

2

____ thirty

____ : ____

3

____ o'clock

____ : ____

4

____ thirty

____ : ____

5

____ o'clock

____ : ____

6

____ o'clock

____ : ____

7

____ thirty

____ : ____

8

____ o'clock

____ : ____

9

____ thirty

____ : ____

Name _____   Lesson 6-2

There are 60 minutes in each hour. As the minute hand moves around the clock face, the hour hand gets closer to the next hour number. Count by fives. Write the minute numbers on the clock.

It is 25 minutes after 3.

The hour hand is between the 3 and the 4.

We can also write 3:25.

The minute hand is on the 5.

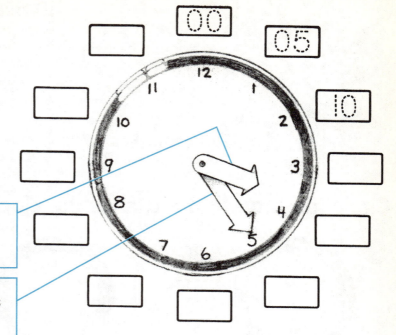

Write each time.

_5_ minutes after _11_

_15_ minutes after _1_

____ minutes after ____

____ minutes after ____

____ minutes after ____

____ minutes after ____

Lesson 6-2 • Telling Time to 5 Minutes

10 minutes after 5

5:10

Circle the time that matches the clock.

1  3:30 (4:30) 5:30

 9:15 10:45 9:45

 12:15 1:15 12:45

2  12:25 1:25 1:35

 12:10 12:50 11:50

 7:00 7:50 7:05

Write each time.

3

3:20

4

_____

5

_____

6

_____

7

_____

8

_____

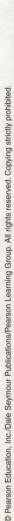

Name _____   **Lesson 6-3**

 Ellen wants to meet a friend 1 hour from now. What time will she meet her friend?

Draw the hour hand.

The time is __7:00__.   1 hour later __8:00__

Write the time shown. Then draw the hour hand to show each new time. Write the new time.

_____ 1 hour later _____   _____ 2 hours later _____

_____ 1 hour earlier _____   _____ 3 hours later _____

_____ 6 hours later _____   _____ 2 hours earlier _____

Lesson 6-3 • Telling Time, Before and After   ninety-seven **97**

Solve.

  Andy fished for 2 hours. What time did he stop? Draw the hour hand.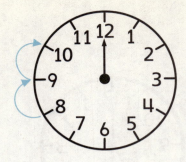

The time is _____.   He stopped at _____.

  Laura played ball for 3 hours. What time did she stop? Draw the hour hand.

The time is _____.   She stopped at _____.

Now Try This!

Roman Numerals are very old. They are still used on some clocks.

Write the Roman Numerals on the clock face.

1	2	3	4	5	6
I	II	III	IV	V	VI
7	8	9	10	11	12
VII	VIII	IX	X	XI	XII

Lesson 6-3 • Telling Time, Before and After

Name _____   **Lesson 6-4**

 Ryan must meet his mother in 30 minutes. What time will it be then? Draw the minute hand.

The time is __1:15__.   30 minutes later __1:45__.

Write the time shown. Then draw the minute hand to show each new time. Write the new time.

        30 minutes later   15 minutes later
__8:15__   __8:45__   _____   _____

        30 minutes later   45 minutes later
_____   _____   _____   _____

        40 minutes later   35 minutes later
_____   _____   _____   _____

Lesson 6-4 • Elapsed Time   ninety-nine **99**

Solve.

1.

Alan started at 3:15. He stopped at 3:30. How long did Alan jump rope? __15__ minutes

2.

Amanda started at _____. She stopped at _____. How long did Amanda jog? _____ minutes

3.

Becky started at _____. She stopped at _____. How long did Becky play tennis? _____ minutes

4.

Royce started at _____. He stopped at _____. How long did Royce ride? _____ minutes

100 one hundred   Lesson 6-4 • Elapsed Time

Name _____ Lesson 6-5

There are __60__ minutes in each hour.
There are __5__ minutes between each hour number.

The minute hand is between the 3 and the 4.
We count 5, 10, 15, 16, 17, 18.
The time is __18__ minutes after __12__ or __12:18__.

Write each time.

_____ minutes after _____

_____

_____ minutes after _____

_____

_____ minutes after _____

_____

_____ minutes after _____

_____

Lesson 6-5 • Telling Time to the Minute

Match the clocks that show the same time.

Write each time.

_____ _____ _____ _____

_____ _____ _____ _____

102 one hundred two Lesson 6-5 • Telling Time to the Minute

Name _____   **Lesson 6-6**

There are __7__ days in a week.

Write the days of the week in order.

1. Sunday, _____ , _____ , _____ ,

   _____ , _____ , _____

Write the day that follows:

2. Thursday, _____
3. Wednesday, _____
4. Monday, _____
5. Sunday, _____

Write the day that comes before:

6. _____ , Friday
7. _____ , Monday
8. _____ , Wednesday
9. _____ , Saturday

Lesson 6-6 • Days, Weeks, and Months   one hundred three **103**

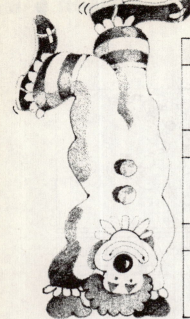

January	February	March	April
May	June	July	August
September	October	November	December

Write the correct month or number on the line.

① There are __12__ months in one year.

② The first month of the year is _____.

③ The last month of the year is _____.

④ The fourth month of the year is _____.

⑤ Which month comes before June? _____

⑥ Which month comes before November? _____

⑦ Which month comes before March? _____

⑧ Which month comes after April? _____

⑨ Which month comes after February? _____

⑩ Which month comes after December? _____

Name _____

Lesson 6-7

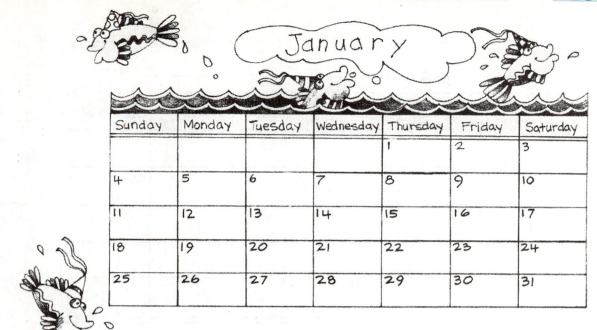

January has 31 days.

Write the dates for each day of the week.

1. Monday: 5 , 12 , ___ , ___

2. Friday: 2 , ___ , ___ , ___ , ___

3. Saturday: ___ , ___ , ___ , ___ , ___

4. Which day of the week does this month begin on? _____

Write the day of the week for each of the following.

5. January fourth: _____

6. January twelfth: _____

7. January nineteenth: _____

8. January thirtieth: _____

9. January twenty-third: _____

10. January fifteenth: _____

Lesson 6-7 • Using a Calendar

Complete the calendar for this month.

_____ Month					_____ Year	
Sunday	Monday	Tuesday	Wednesday	Thursday	Friday	Saturday

1. How many days are in this month? _____

2. _____ is the first day of the month.

3. _____ is the last day of the month.

4. There are _____ holidays in this month.

How many of each of the following days are there in this month?

5. Sundays _____

6. Mondays _____

7. Tuesdays _____

8. Wednesdays _____

9. Thursdays _____

10. Fridays _____

11. Saturdays _____

Name _____

Lesson 6-8

I penny
I cent
1¢

I nickel
5 cents
5¢

I dime
10 cents
10¢

Count the money. Write the amount.

1)

   5   10   15   16   17   18   19   19¢

2)

   ___ ___ ___ ___ ___ ___

3)

   ___ ___ ___ ___ ___ ___ ___

4)

   ___ ___ ___ ___ ___ ___ ___ ___

Lesson 6-8 • Counting Money Through Dimes

Circle the coins needed to buy each item.

Name _____   **Lesson 6-9**

1 quarter

5 nickels

2 dimes 1 nickel

25 cents 25¢

25 cents 25¢

25 cents 25¢

Count the money. Write the amount.

            67¢

25 35 45 55 60 65 66 67

2   ____

____ ____ ____ ____ ____ ____

3   ____

4   ____

____ ____ ____ ____ ____ ____ ____ ____

Lesson 6-9 • Counting Money Through Quarters

Is there enough money to buy each item? Circle yes or no.

1.

   (Yes) / No

2.

   Yes / No

3.

   Yes / No

Now Try This!

Find five ways to make 25¢.

1. _1_ quarter
2. _2_ dimes _1_ nickel
3. ___ dime ___ nickels
4. ___ nickels
5. ___ pennies

Find five ways to make 31¢.

1. _1_ quarter, _1_ nickel, _1_ penny
2. _____
3. _____
4. _____
5. _____

110 one hundred ten

Lesson 6-9 • Counting Money Through Quarters

Name _____ Lesson 6-10

1 half-dollar
50 cents
50¢

2 quarters
50 cents
50¢

5 dimes
50 cents
50¢

Count the money. Write the amount.

10   20   25   25 ¢

_____

_____

_____

____ quarters = ____ half-dollar

_____

____ nickels = ____ half-dollar

**Count the money. Write the amount.
Is there enough money to buy each item? Circle yes or no.**

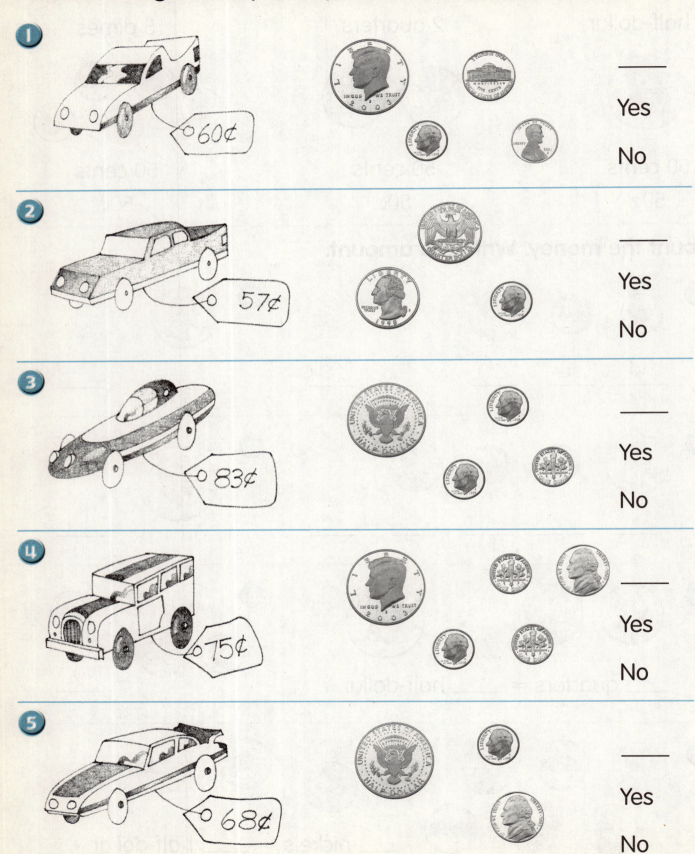

112 one hundred twelve   Lesson 6-10 • Counting Money Through Half-Dollars

Name _____ **Lesson 6-11**

1¢	5¢	10¢	25¢	50¢	100¢

$0.01	$0.05	$0.10	$0.25	$0.50	$1.00

Count the money. Write each amount in two ways.

1

100 ¢
$1.00

2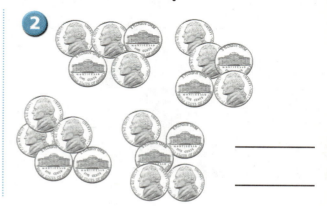

_____
_____

3

_____
_____

4

_____
_____

5

_____
_____

6

_____
_____

Lesson 6-11 • Counting Money Through Dollars

Count the money. Write each amount in two ways.

1.    175¢ / $1.75

2.     _____ / _____

3.    _____ / _____

4.    _____ / _____

5.   _____ / _____

6.    _____ / _____

7.    _____ / _____

8.    _____ / _____

Name _____

Problem Solving
Lesson 6-12

Count the money. Cross out the coins spent. Solve.

1

Dina has __52¢__.

She spent 41¢.

She has __11¢__ left.

2

Robbie has _____.

He spent 67¢.

He has _____ left.

3

Pedro has _____.

He spent 55¢.

He has _____ left.

4

Katie has _____.

She spent 62¢.

She has _____ left.

5

Sherry has _____.

She spent 58¢.

She has _____ left.

6

Nathan has _____.

He spent 93¢.

He has _____ left.

Count the money. Cross out the money spent. Solve.

①

Chan has $ 1.28 .

He spent $1.02.

He has 26¢ left.

②

Julie has _____ .

She spent $2.32.

She has _____ left.

③

Lori has _____ .

She spent $1.16.

She has _____ left.

④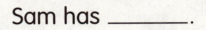

Sam has _____ .

He spent 17¢.

He has _____ left.

Now Try This!

① 50¢ is the same as

____ half-dollar

____ quarters

____ dimes

____ nickels

____ pennies

② $1.00 is the same as

____ half-dollars

____ quarters

____ dimes

____ nickels

____ pennies

116 one hundred sixteen   Lesson 6-12 • Problem Solving: Act It Out

Name _____

Chapter 6 Test

Write each time.

1  _____ o'clock

_____ : _____

2  _____ minutes after _____

_____

3  The time is _____.

Sheila skated for 2 hours. What time did she stop? Draw the hour hand.
She stopped at _____.

4 What day comes after Thursday?

_____

5 What month comes after June?

_____

6 Count the money. Write the amount.

___ ___ ___ ___ ___

___

Count the money. Cross out the money spent. Solve.

7

Fran has _____.

She spent 75¢.

She has _____ left.

8

Emil has _____.

He spent $1.05.

He has _____ left.

Chapter 6 • Test   one hundred seventeen **117**

Cumulative Assessment

Add or subtract.

1.
```
  7      8       5      14      10      15      12
+ 4    + 7     + 5    − 6     − 9     − 6     − 5
```

2.
```
 11     13       6       8      16       8       9
− 6    − 6     + 6     + 5    − 8     + 6     + 9
```

Write the number.

3. _____

Count by ones. Write the numbers.

4. 96, 97, 98, ____, ____, ____, ____, ____

5. 308, 309, ____, ____, ____, ____, ____

6. 896, 897, ____, ____, ____, ____, ____

Write the time.

7.

_____

Count the money. Cross out the coins spent. Solve.

8.

Carl has _____.

He spent 66¢. He has _____ left.

118 one hundred eighteen

GET READY,
GET SET,
GET ON . . .

WATCH FOR . . .

MODEL PROBLEM
Work through the problem with your teacher.

GETTING STARTED
Try the new math skill. Ask questions.

PRACTICE
Complete the problems to practice the new skill.

PROBLEM SOLVING
Solve word problems using the math skills you have learned.

NOW TRY THIS!
Have fun with mathematics.

Name _____

Addition With 2-Digit Numbers

Chapter 7

Lesson 7-1

Adding 2-Digit and 1-Digit Numbers

Anita took 32 pictures on Monday.
She took 4 pictures on Tuesday.
How many pictures did Anita take?

We are looking for the total number of pictures that Anita took.

Anita took ____ pictures on Monday.

She took ____ pictures on Tuesday.

To find the total, we add ____ and ____.

Add the ones first.

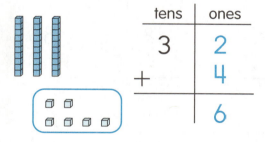

tens	ones
3	2
+	4
	6

Add the tens.

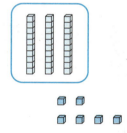

tens	ones
3	2
+	4
3	6

Anita took ____ pictures.

Getting Started

Add.

1.
tens	ones
4	4
+	3

2.
tens	ones
7	3
+	5

3.
tens	ones
2	1
+	6

4. 83
   + 1

5. 13
   + 2

6. 57
   + 2

7. 95
   + 1

8. 64
   + 4

9. 33
   + 2

Lesson 7-1 • Adding 2-Digit and 1-Digit Numbers

Practice

Add.

1.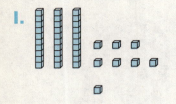

tens	ones
3	7
+	1

2.
tens	ones
5	2
+	5

3.
tens	ones
4	2
+	5

4.
tens	ones
6	5
+	3

5.
tens	ones
5	2
+	7

6.
tens	ones
2	2
+	1

7. 70
  + 9

8. 43
  + 6

9. 55
  + 1

10. 23
  + 2

11. 18
  + 1

12. 86
  + 3

13. 31
  + 7

14. 14
  + 3

15. 93
  + 6

16. 84
  + 1

17. 44
  + 4

18. 63
  + 4

Problem Solving

Solve.

19. Hector had 35 pennies. Alan gave him 3 more. How many pennies does Hector have now?

_____ pennies

20. Joyce ran for 21 minutes. Then she ran laps for 8 minutes. How many minutes did Joyce run?

_____ minutes

Name _____

Lesson 7-2

Adding With Regrouping

Andrew hopped 26 times on his left foot and 8 times on his right foot. How many times did Andrew hop?

We want to find out how many times Andrew hopped.

Andrew hopped _____ times on his left foot.

He hopped _____ times on his right foot.

To find the total number of hops, we add _____ and _____.

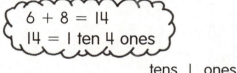

Add the ones first. Regroup if needed.

$6 + 8 = 14$
$14 = 1$ ten 4 ones

tens	ones
1	
2	6
+	8
	4

Add the tens.

$1 + 2$ tens $= 3$ tens

tens	ones
1	
2	6
+	8
3	4

Andrew hopped _____ times.

Getting Started

Add. Regroup if needed.

1.
tens	ones
3	7
+	5

2. 28
  + 9
  ----

3. 35
  + 4
  ----

4. 77
  + 3

Lesson 7-2 • Adding With Regrouping

one hundred twenty-three **123**

Practice

Add. Regroup if needed.

1.
tens	ones
3	7
+	6

2.
tens	ones
5	3
+	9

3. 34 + 5

4. 65 + 6

5. 83 + 9

6. 62 + 7

7. 29 + 5

8. 56 + 8

9. 23 + 6

10. 39 + 3

11. 28 + 6

12. 61 + 8

13. 75 + 9

14. 57 + 4

Now Try This!

Write the missing number.

It's Algebra!

1. 34 + ☐ = 36

2. 17 + ☐ = 19

3. 16 + ☐ = 20

4. 31 + ☐ = 39

5. 62 + ☐ = 67

6. 23 + ☐ = 30

7. 35 + ☐ = 41

8. 63 + ☐ = 72

9. 46 + ☐ = 53

10. 57 + ☐ = 65

Lesson 7-3

Adding 2-Digit Numbers

The Bowsers took a vacation. They drove from Boneville to Pooch City on Monday. On Tuesday they drove from Pooch City to Wagtown. How many miles did they drive?

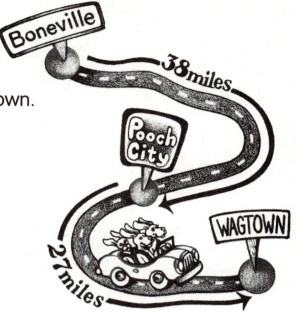

We want to find out the total number of miles they drove.

On Monday they drove _____ miles.

On Tuesday they drove _____ miles.

To find how far they drove, we add _____ and _____.

Add the ones first. Regroup if needed.

8 + 7 = 15
15 = 1 ten 5 ones

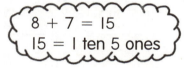

tens	ones
3	8
+ 2	7
	5

Add the tens.

1 + 3 + 2 tens = 6 tens

tens	ones
3	8
+ 2	7
6	5

The Bowsers drove _____ miles.

Getting Started

Add. Regroup if needed.

1.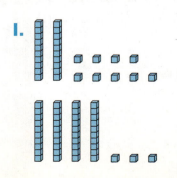

tens	ones
2	9
+ 4	3

2. 27
   + 64

3. 14
   + 73

4. 61
   + 19

Practice

Add. Regroup if needed.

1.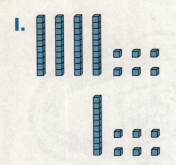

tens	ones
4	6
+1	6

2.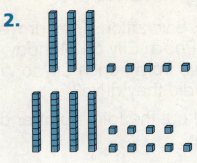

tens	ones
3	5
+4	9

3. 36 + 47
4. 52 + 45
5. 35 + 16
6. 53 + 46
7. 37 + 48
8. 52 + 18

9. 60 + 25
10. 16 + 17
11. 29 + 44
12. 48 + 23
13. 56 + 39
14. 19 + 31

15. 28 + 37
16. 46 + 45
17. 18 + 68
18. 25 + 14
19. 73 + 17
20. 49 + 38

Problem Solving

Solve.

21. The cafeteria sold 35 ham sandwiches and 25 cheese sandwiches. How many sandwiches were sold?

_____ sandwiches

22. The cafeteria sold 45 cartons of milk and 29 cartons of orange juice. How many cartons were sold?

_____ cartons

Name ______________________________

Adding Multiples of 10

Manuel and Christy wanted to see how many times they could bounce a basketball without missing. What is the total number of times they bounced the ball?

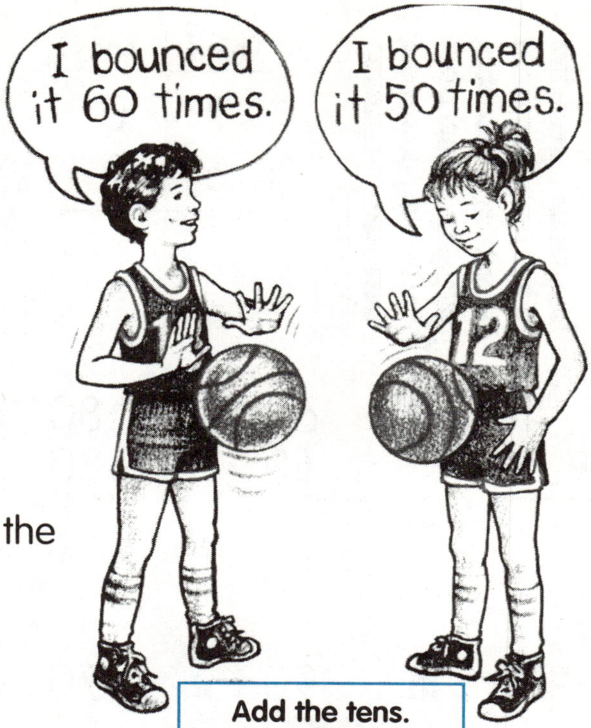

We want to know the total number of times they bounced the ball.

Manuel bounced the ball _____ times.

Christy bounced the ball _____ times.

To find how many times they bounced the ball, we add _____ and _____.

Add the ones first.

	tens	ones
	6	0
+	5	0
		0

Add the tens. Regroup if needed.

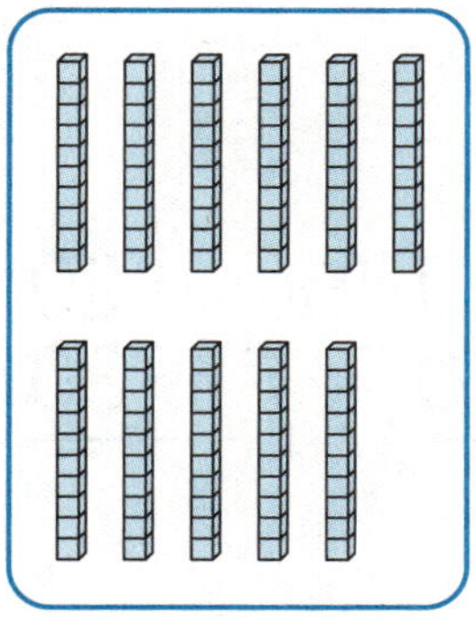

	tens	ones
	6	0
+	5	0
	11	0

11 tens = 1 hundred 1 ten

They bounced the ball _____ times.

Getting Started

Add. Regroup if needed.

1.

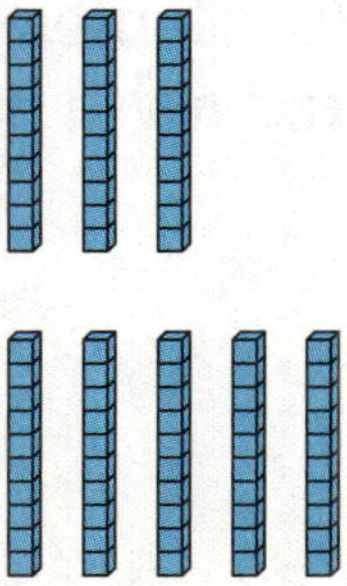

	tens	ones
	3	0
+	5	0

2. $20 + 90$

3. $50 + 50$

4. $90 + 90$

Practice

Add. Regroup if needed.

1.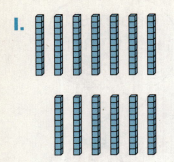

tens	ones
7	0
+ 6	0

2.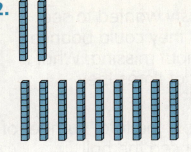

tens	ones
2	0
+ 9	0

3. 40 + 30

4. 60 + 60

5. 80 + 80

6. 30 + 50

7. 90 + 90

8. 50 + 50

9. 50 + 40

10. 90 + 50

11. 70 + 80

12. 10 + 90

13. 80 + 40

14. 70 + 50

15. 80 + 90

16. 90 + 70

17. 20 + 30

18. 70 + 60

19. 20 + 80

20. 60 + 50

Problem Solving

Solve.

21. Phil took 30 steps to the door and 30 steps back. How many steps did Phil take?

_____ steps

22. Myra rode her bike for 40 minutes. She played ball for 70 minutes. How many minutes did Myra play?

_____ minutes

Name _____

Lesson 7-5

Finding 3-Digit Sums

Some children collect baseball cards. How many cards did Morris and Sandi collect together?

Baseball Cards Collected
Morris — 58 cards
Sandi — 67 cards
Del — 51 cards

We are looking for the total number of cards collected by Morris and Sandi.

Morris has _____ cards.

Sandi has _____ cards.

To find how many cards Morris and Sandi have, we

add _____ and _____.

Add the ones. Regroup if needed.

8 + 7 = 15
15 = 1 ten 5 ones

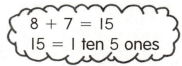

tens	ones
1	
5	8
+ 6	7
	5

Add the tens. Regroup if needed.

12 tens = 1 hundred 2 tens

tens	ones
1	
5	8
+ 6	7
12	5

Morris and Sandi have _____ cards.

Getting Started

Add. Regroup if needed.

1.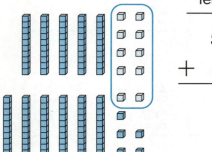

tens	ones
5	7
+ 8	5

2. 38
  + 85

3. 27
  + 58

4. 79
  + 65

Lesson 7-5 • Finding 3-Digit Sums   one hundred twenty-nine **129**

Practice

Add. Regroup if needed.

1.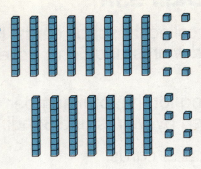

tens	ones
2	9
+ 7	4

2.

tens	ones
8	8
+ 7	7

3. 34
  + 23

4. 85
  + 57

5. 29
  + 76

6. 16
  + 37

7. 43
  + 44

8. 91
  + 26

9. 35
  + 45

10. 67
  + 78

11. 38
  + 38

12. 75
  + 75

13. 41
  + 99

14. 27
  + 98

15. 57
  + 23

16. 56
  + 65

17. 99
  + 99

18. 65
  + 85

19. 36
  + 55

20. 43
  + 75

21. 25
  + 63

22. 69
  + 32

23. 47
  + 77

24. 38
  + 95

25. 67
  + 27

26. 83
  + 79

130 one hundred thirty

Lesson 7-5 • Finding 3-Digit Sums

Name _____

Lesson 7-6

Adding Money

Gene went shopping for gifts. He bought a bag of marbles and a yo-yo. How much did he pay?

We want to find out how much Gene paid for the gifts.

The bag of marbles cost _____.

The yo-yo cost _____.

To find the total cost, we

add _____ and _____.

| Add the ones first. Regroup if needed. | Add the dimes. Regroup if needed. |

```
   1                    1
  48¢                  48¢
+ 75¢                + 75¢
-----                -----
   3¢                 123¢
```

123¢ = $1.23

The total cost of the gifts is _____.

Getting Started

Add. Then write each answer in dollar notation.

1. 96¢
  + 25¢
  -----

2. 37¢
  + 88¢
  -----

3. 56¢
  + 38¢
  -----

4. 75¢
  + 25¢

Lesson 7-6 • Adding Money

Practice

Add. Then write each answer in dollar notation.

1. 30¢
    + 30¢
    ─────

2. 45¢
    + 56¢
    ─────

3. 62¢
    + 76¢
    ─────

4. 79¢
    + 75¢
    ─────

5. 99¢
    + 8¢
    ─────

6. 81¢
    + 93¢
    ─────

7. 84¢
    + 68¢
    ─────

8. 91¢
    + 65¢
    ─────

9. 87¢
    + 26¢
    ─────

10. 58¢
    + 82¢
    ─────

11. 40¢
    + 87¢
    ─────

12. 55¢
    + 98¢
    ─────

13. 90¢
    + 71¢
    ─────

14. 73¢
    + 68¢
    ─────

15. 64¢
    + 63¢
    ─────

Problem Solving

Solve. Then write each answer in dollar notation.

16. Lu had 50¢. She earned 75¢ raking leaves. How much money does she have now?

17. Walt bought one book for 89¢ and another book for 95¢. How much money did he spend?

Name _____

Problem Solving: Make an Organized List

Problem Solving Lesson 7-7

It's Algebra!

Joe has $1.00. He buys a pencil that costs 75¢. He gets 25¢ back as change. How many different ways can Joe get 25¢?

The chart below shows three ways.

 = 25¢   = 10¢   = 5¢   = 1¢

				Amount
1				25¢
		5		
			25	

Getting Started

Make a chart to answer the questions.

1. Using only dimes and nickels, how can you make 25¢?

2. Using only dimes and pennies, how can you make 25¢?

3. Using only nickels and pennies, how can you make 25¢?

4. Using dimes, nickels, and pennies, how can you make 25¢?

Lesson 7-7 • Problem Solving: Make an Organized List

one hundred thirty-three **133**

Practice

Complete the chart to answer the questions.

 = 25¢   ◯ = 10¢   ◯ = 5¢   ◯ = 1¢

1. Roberta has one of each coin above. If she picks 2 coins, what amounts can she make?

Quarter	Dime	Nickel	Penny	Amount
1	1	0	0	35¢

2. If Roberta picks 3 coins, what amounts can she make?

3. How many different amounts can Roberta make in all?

   _____ different amounts

Solve.

4. Ling has $1.00. She buys a ruler for 60¢. How much change does she receive?

5. Ling did not receive any pennies in the change. List the combinations of change she could have received.

Quarter	Dime	Nickel	Amount

Name _____

Chapter 7 Test

Add. Regroup if needed.

1. 83 + 5
2. 35 + 9
3. 86 + 7
4. 80 + 50
5. 30 + 70
6. 90 + 40

7. 57 + 31
8. 65 + 29
9. 34 + 82
10. 76 + 77
11. 99 + 99
12. 42 + 38

13. 16 + 7
14. 56 + 68
15. 30 + 80
16. 76 + 21
17. 64 + 4
18. 43 + 17

19. 45 + 45
20. 59 + 84
21. 38 + 37
22. 27 + 9
23. 98 + 3
24. 75 + 83

Add. Then write each answer in dollar notation.

25. 68¢ + 7¢
26. 70¢ + 50¢
27. 64¢ + 24¢
28. 75¢ + 18¢
29. 96¢ + 89¢

_____ _____ _____ _____ _____

Solve.

30. There were 65 girls and 77 boys on the skating rink. How many children were skating?

    _____ children

31. Cleve has 85¢. Lu Ann has 98¢. How much money do they have in all?

    _____

Chapter 7 • Test

one hundred thirty-five **135**

Cumulative Assessment

Circle the letter of the correct answer.

1.   8
     + 7

   a. 16
   b. 15
   c. 14
   d. NG

2. 9 + 3

   a. 10
   b. 16
   c. 12
   d. NG

3.   15
     − 6

   a. 9
   b. 7
   c. 6
   d. NG

4.   13
     − 7

   a. 5
   b. 7
   c. 6
   d. NG

5.

   a. 3:10
   b. 2:15
   c. 2:03
   d. NG

6.

   a. $3.45
   b. $3.35
   c. $3.40
   d. NG

7. What is the value of the 6 in 267?

   a. hundreds
   b. tens
   c. ones
   d. NG

8. What is the value of the 7 in 750?

   a. hundreds
   b. tens
   c. ones
   d. NG

9. 364 ◯ 446

   a. >
   b. <

10.   37
      + 58

    a. 94
    b. 85
    c. 95
    d. NG

11.   60
      + 60

    a. 12
    b. 102
    c. 130
    d. NG

12.   35
      + 7

    a. 42
    b. 32
    c. 47
    d. NG

13.   75
      + 88

    a. 153
    b. 165
    c. 163
    d. NG

score

Chapter 8

Subtraction with 2-Digit Numbers

Lesson 8-1

Subtracting 2-Digit Numbers

Gary had 47 fish in his aquarium.
He gave 15 fish to Sun Li.
How many fish does he have left?

We want to know how many fish Gary has left.

Gary had ____ fish.

He gave ____ fish to Sun Li.

To find the number of fish he has left, we subtract ____ from ____.

Subtract the ones first.

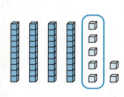

tens	ones
4	7
− 1	5
	2

Subtract the tens.

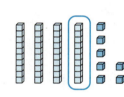

tens	ones
4	7
− 1	5
3	2

Gary has ____ fish left.

Getting Started

Subtract.

1. | tens | ones |
    |------|------|
    | 6 | 7 |
    | − 2 | 5 |

2. | tens | ones |
    |------|------|
    | 9 | 6 |
    | − 4 | 3 |

3. | tens | ones |
    |------|------|
    | 5 | 5 |
    | − 3 | 1 |

4. | tens | ones |
    |------|------|
    | 7 | 8 |
    | − | 5 |

5. 97
    − 22

6. 42
    − 11

7. 28
    − 3

8. 79
    − 46

9. 48
    − 28

10. 37
    − 10

Lesson 8-1 • Subtracting 2-Digit Numbers

Practice
Subtract.

1.	tens	ones
	8	3
−	2	1

2.	tens	ones
	5	7
−	4	1

3.	tens	ones
	6	8
−	6	4

4.	tens	ones
	2	9
−		9

5. 78
   − 52

6. 35
   − 2

7. 46
   − 22

8. 99
   − 4

9. 76
   − 6

10. 87
   − 83

11. 47
   − 31

12. 75
   − 55

13. 18
   − 7

14. 88
   − 46

15. 36
   − 26

16. 50
   − 20

17. 56
   − 54

18. 22
   − 1

19. 77
   − 50

20. 96
   − 36

21. 49
   − 2

22. 58
   − 30

Problem Solving
Solve.

23. At the bake sale, they sold 48 blueberry muffins and 36 bran muffins. How many more blueberry muffins were sold?

_____ blueberry muffins

24. The sale started with 28 loaves of bread. They had 5 left. How many loaves of bread were sold?

_____ loaves

138 one hundred thirty-eight • Lesson 8-1 • Subtracting 2-Digit Numbers

Name _____

Lesson 8-2

Regrouping a Ten to Subtract

The pet store had 34 puppies for sale. The store sold 8 puppies. How many puppies are left?

There were _____ puppies for sale.

The store sold _____ puppies.

To find out how many are left, we subtract _____ from _____.

REMEMBER Subtract the ones first.

Do you need more ones?	Regroup 1 ten to get 10 ones.	Subtract the ones.	Subtract the tens.
4 − 8 = ? Yes, you need more ones.	Now there are 2 tens and 14 ones.	14 − 8 = 6	2 − 0 = 2

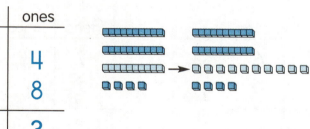

tens	ones
3	4
−	8
	?

tens	ones
2	14
3̸	4̸
−	8
	6

tens	ones
2	14
3̸	4̸
−	8
2	6

The pet store has _____ puppies left.

Getting Started

**Do you need more ones? Circle yes or no.
Then subtract and regroup if needed.**

1.
tens	ones	
5	6	Yes
−	9	No

2.
tens	ones	
2	2	Yes
−	8	No

3.
tens	ones	
6	8	Yes
−	7	No

Lesson 8-2 • Regrouping a Ten to Subtract

Practice

**Do you need more ones? Circle yes or no.
Then subtract and regroup if needed.**

1. | tens | ones |
   |------|------|
   | 6 | 8 |
   | − | 5 |

   Yes No

2. | tens | ones |
   |------|------|
   | 5 | 2 |
   | − | 8 |

   Yes No

3. | tens | ones |
   |------|------|
   | 7 | 7 |
   | − | 7 |

   Yes No

4. | tens | ones |
   |------|------|
   | 8 | 0 |
   | − | 3 |

   Yes No

5. | tens | ones |
   |------|------|
   | 7 | 9 |
   | − | 6 |

   Yes No

6. | tens | ones |
   |------|------|
   | 3 | 3 |
   | − | 4 |

   Yes No

7. | tens | ones |
   |------|------|
   | 5 | 7 |
   | − | 8 |

   Yes No

8. | tens | ones |
   |------|------|
   | 4 | 6 |
   | − | 9 |

   Yes No

9. | tens | ones |
   |------|------|
   | 7 | 3 |
   | − | 1 |

   Yes No

Problem Solving

Solve.

10. Charlie collects eggs on his farm. One day he gathered 87 white eggs and 9 brown eggs. How many more white eggs did he collect?

    _____ white eggs

11. Debra picked 24 ears of corn. Father cooked 9 ears for dinner. How many ears of corn were not cooked?

    _____ ears of corn

Name _____   **Lesson 8-3**

Subtracting With Regrouping

Annie collects stuffed animals. She must take 17 of them to school for a display. How many are left at home?

We want to know how many stuffed animals she left at home.

Annie has ____ stuffed animals.

She is taking ____ stuffed animals to school.

To find how many stuffed animals she left at home, we subtract ____ from ____.

REMEMBER Subtract the ones first.

Do you need more ones?	Regroup 1 ten to get 10 ones.	Subtract the ones.	Subtract the tens.
$6 - 7 = ?$ Yes, you need more ones.	Now there are 2 tens and 16 ones.	$16 - 7 = 9$	$2 - 1 = 1$

tens	ones
3	6
− 1	7
	?

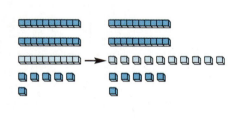

tens	ones
2	16
3̸	6̸
− 1	7
	9

tens	ones
2	16
3̸	6̸
− 1	7
1	9

Annie left ____ stuffed animals at home.

Getting Started

Subtract. Regroup if needed.

1.
tens	ones
9	3
− 5	9

2.
tens	ones
6	2
− 3	6

3.
tens	ones
8	4
− 2	9

4.
tens	ones
8	8
− 1	8

Lesson 8-3 • Subtracting With Regrouping   one hundred forty-one **141**

Practice

Subtract. Regroup if needed.

1.
tens	ones
5	7
−2	3

2.
tens	ones
8	0
−3	0

3.
tens	ones
8	1
−1	2

4.
tens	ones
4	2
−1	7

5.
tens	ones
8	3
−5	5

6.
tens	ones
5	0
−2	9

7.
tens	ones
9	0
−2	0

8.
tens	ones
7	5
−4	5

9.
tens	ones
5	5
	6

10.
tens	ones
7	9
−3	0

11.
tens	ones
9	6
−3	8

12.
tens	ones
6	7
−4	9

Now Try This!

Stacey has 15¢. How many pennies, nickels, and dimes would make 15¢ if she had the following:

1. 2 coins _____
2. 3 coins _____
3. 6 coins _____
4. 7 coins _____

142 one hundred forty-two

Lesson 8-3 • Subtracting With Regrouping

Name _____   Lesson 8-4

Review Subtracting With Regrouping

Rhoda collected 55 shells.
Diana collected 39 shells.
How many more shells did Rhoda collect?

We want to know how many more shells Rhoda has.

Rhoda has ____ shells.

Diana has ____ shells.

To find how many more shells Rhoda has, we subtract ____ from ____.

REMEMBER Subtract the ones first.

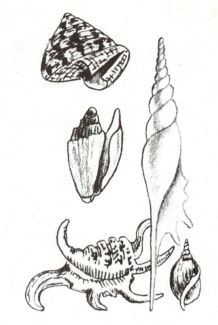

| Do you need more ones? | Regroup 1 ten to get 10 ones. | Subtract the ones. | Subtract the tens. |

5 − 9 = ?
Yes, you need more ones.

Now there are 4 tens and 15 ones.

15 − 9 = 6

4 − 3 = 1

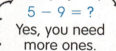

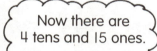

tens	ones
4	15
5̸	5̸
− 3	9
	6

tens	ones
4	15
5̸	5̸
− 3	9
1	6

Rhoda has ____ more shells than Diana.

Getting Started

Subtract. Regroup if needed.

1.
tens	ones
6	3
− 2	8

2.
tens	ones
8	7
− 3	4

3. 75
   − 12

4. 52
   − 25

5. 90
   − 52

Lesson 8-4 • Review Subtracting With Regrouping

Practice
Subtract.

1. | tens | ones |
|---|---|
| 6 | 8 |
| −2 | 3 |

2. | tens | ones |
|---|---|
| 7 | 1 |
| −3 | 9 |

3. | tens | ones |
|---|---|
| 5 | 2 |
| −2 | 6 |

4. | tens | ones |
|---|---|
| 8 | 5 |
| −2 | 5 |

5. 57 − 23
6. 75 − 29
7. 53 − 46
8. 79 − 30
9. 50 − 8
10. 32 − 18

11. 73 − 50
12. 57 − 45
13. 81 − 15
14. 77 − 39
15. 31 − 17
16. 64 − 9

17. 83 − 33
18. 61 − 34
19. 60 − 20
20. 77 − 18
21. 82 − 55
22. 53 − 47

Problem Solving
Solve.

23. Martha had 80¢. She lost 35¢. How much was left?

24. Allan earned 68¢ on Friday. He earned 25¢ on Saturday. How much more did he earn on Friday?

Name _____   **Lesson 8-5**

Practice Subtracting With Regrouping

Anna had fun riding her bike. How many more blocks did she ride the first week than the second week?

Anna
1st week 61 blocks
2nd week 43 blocks
3rd week 63 blocks

We want to know how many more blocks she rode her bike the first week than the second week.

Anna rode her bike _____ blocks the first week.

She rode her bike _____ blocks the second week.

To find how many more blocks she rode her bike the first week than the second week, we subtract _____ from _____.

REMEMBER Subtract the ones first.

Subtract the ones. Regroup if needed.	Subtract the tens.
$^{5}\cancel{6}^{11}\cancel{1}$ -43 8	$^{5}\cancel{6}^{11}\cancel{1}$ -43 18

Anna rode her bike _____ more blocks the first week than the second week.

Getting Started

Subtract. Regroup if needed.

1.	2.	3.	4.	5.	6.
90 − 49	87 − 23	45 − 18	67 − 47	54 − 39	90 − 40

Practice

Subtract. Regroup if needed.

1. 90 − 50
2. 65 − 35
3. 73 − 40
4. 65 − 9
5. 51 − 27
6. 86 − 28

7. 75 − 41
8. 48 − 24
9. 34 − 17
10. 56 − 37
11. 83 − 55
12. 51 − 19

13. 62 − 28
14. 97 − 65
15. 80 − 52
16. 45 − 25
17. 37 − 18
18. 64 − 57

19. 83 − 48
20. 77 − 56
21. 44 − 14
22. 32 − 16
23. 58 − 25
24. 33 − 18

25. 92 − 34
26. 83 − 71
27. 41 − 26
28. 94 − 57
29. 88 − 44
30. 71 − 29

Problem Solving

Solve.

31. There were 35 bikes in a race. 17 bikes got flat tires. How many bikes did not get flat tires?

    _____ bikes

32. There were 25 prizes given. 19 children got bike lights. How many children got other prizes?

    _____ children

Lesson 8-6

Using Addition to Check Subtraction

The Pet Shoppe had 55 birds.
It sold 27 of them.
How many birds are left?

We want to know how many birds are left.

The store had ____ birds.

It sold ____ birds.

To find how many are left, we subtract ____ from ____.

Subtract the ones first. Regroup if needed.	Subtract the tens.	Check by adding.

$$\begin{array}{r} \overset{4}{\cancel{5}}\overset{15}{\cancel{5}} \\ -\ 2\ 7 \\ \hline 8 \end{array}$$

$$\begin{array}{r} \overset{4}{\cancel{5}}\overset{15}{\cancel{5}} \\ -\ 2\ 7 \\ \hline 2\ 8 \end{array}$$

(These should be the same.)

$$\begin{array}{r} 2\ 8 \\ +\ 2\ 7 \\ \hline 5\ 5 \end{array}$$

The Pet Shoppe has ____ birds left.

Getting Started

Subtract. Regroup if needed. Check your answers.

1. $\begin{array}{r} 37 \\ -15 \\ \hline 22 \end{array}$ → $\begin{array}{r} 22 \\ +15 \\ \hline 37 \end{array}$

2. $\begin{array}{r} 81 \\ -43 \\ \hline \end{array}$

3. $\begin{array}{r} 75 \\ -39 \\ \hline \end{array}$

4. $\begin{array}{r} 43 \\ -17 \\ \hline \end{array}$

5. $\begin{array}{r} 64 \\ -41 \\ \hline \end{array}$

6. $\begin{array}{r} 57 \\ -28 \\ \hline \end{array}$

Practice

Subtract. Regroup if needed. Check your answers.

1. 75 − 25
2. 61 − 27
3. 38 − 13
4. 53 − 36
5. 85 − 59
6. 67 − 39
7. 42 − 15
8. 95 − 58
9. 51 − 43
10. 99 − 69
11. 64 − 25
12. 77 − 48

Now Try This!

It's Algebra!

Solve.

1. Subtract two numbers. One number is 25. The answer is 50. What is the other number?

2. Subtract two numbers. The greater number is 60. The answer is 45. What is the other number?

Lesson 8-7

Subtracting Money

Alice saved 85¢ to buy a kite. After buying one kite, how much money does she have left?

We want to know how much money she has left.

Alice saved ____.

She spends ____.

To find how much money she has left, we subtract ____ from ____.

| Subtract the pennies first. Regroup if needed. | Subtract the dimes. |

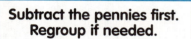

Alice has ____ left.

Getting Started

Subtract. Regroup if needed.

1. 36¢ − 15¢
2. 47¢ − 19¢
3. 75¢ − 38¢
4. 78¢ − 56¢
5. 91¢ − 73¢

6. 83¢ − 42¢
7. 90¢ − 53¢
8. 84¢ − 58¢
9. 97¢ − 57¢
10. 46¢ − 28¢

Practice

Subtract. Regroup if needed. Check your answers.

1. 70¢ − 30¢
2. 90¢ − 21¢
3. 84¢ − 27¢
4. 99¢ − 66¢
5. 51¢ − 23¢

6. 98¢ − 29¢
7. 45¢ − 22¢
8. 57¢ − 39¢
9. 75¢ − 50¢
10. 60¢ − 41¢

11. 27¢ − 9¢
12. 65¢ − 35¢
13. 80¢ − 50¢
14. 52¢ − 7¢
15. 45¢ − 36¢

16. 48¢ − 15¢
17. 73¢ − 55¢
18. 64¢ − 17¢
19. 35¢ − 15¢
20. 96¢ − 77¢

Problem Solving

Solve.

21. Li saved 95¢. She bought some crayons for 75¢. How much money does she have left?

22. Lonnie saved 45¢. He bought a truck for 35¢. How much money does he have now?

Name _____

Problem Solving
Lesson 8-8

Problem Solving: Make and Use a Graph

Mrs. Peach's class is taking a vote on its favorite kinds of fruits. The students are going to make a bar graph to show the results of their vote.

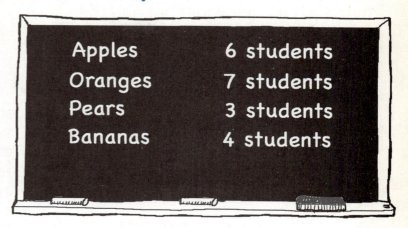

Use the information on the board to help Mrs. Peach and her class complete the bar graph. Then answer each question.

There are _____ kinds of fruit.
The graph needs _____ rows.

The most number of fruits is _____.
The least number of fruits is _____.

The graph can go from 0 to 10.
The title of the graph is _____.

Color in the boxes for each fruit.

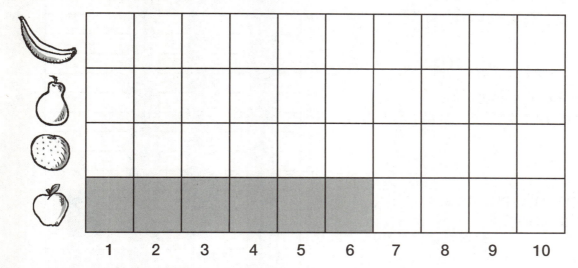

Use the graph to find the answers.

1. How many students picked bananas as their favorite fruit? _____

2. Which fruit got the most votes? _____

3. Which fruit got the least votes? _____

Practice

Maria showed a list of four pets to her friends at school. She asked each friend to pick a favorite pet and then made a graph of their choices.

Use Maria's graph to find the answers.

1. _____ children chose a cat.

2. _____ children chose a dog.

3. _____ children chose a bird.

4. _____ children chose a rabbit.

5. How many children chose a cat or a dog?
   _____

6. How many more children chose a dog than a cat?
   _____

7. How many children chose a bird or a rabbit?
   _____

8. How many children chose a dog or a rabbit?
   _____

9. How many more children chose a cat than a rabbit?
   _____

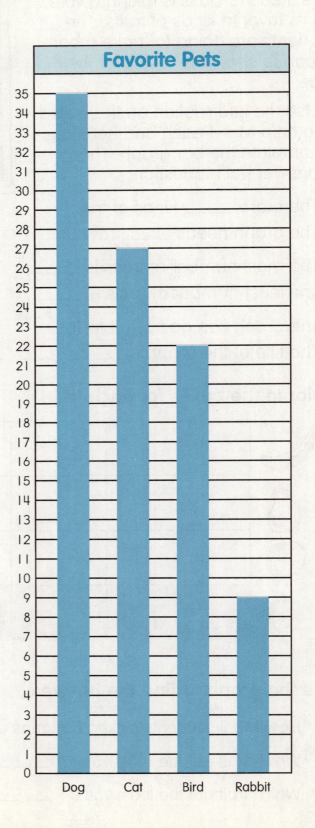

Favorite Pets

152 one hundred fifty-two   Lesson 8-8 • Problem Solving: Make and Use a Graph

Name _____

Chapter 8 Test

Subtract. Regroup if needed.

1. 25 − 3
2. 35 − 8
3. 71 − 5
4. 55 − 9

5. 80 − 30
6. 90 − 30
7. 60 − 20
8. 85 − 31

9. 45 − 17
10. 71 − 53
11. 64 − 19
12. 97 − 29

13. 83 − 15
14. 98 − 75
15. 81 − 67
16. 35 − 19

17. 75¢ − 25¢
18. 65¢ − 48¢
19. 92¢ − 55¢
20. 73¢ − 15¢

Solve.

21. Pat saved 35 marbles. She gave Dino 16 of them. How many marbles did she have left?

    _____ marbles

22. The pet store had 75 goldfish. It sold 39 of them. How many goldfish were left?

    _____ goldfish

Cumulative Assessment

Circle the letter of the correct answer.

1.
   15
   − 9

   a. 24
   b. 6
   c. 14
   d. NG

2.
   7
   + 4

   a. 11
   b. 3
   c. 4
   d. NG

3.

   a. 81¢
   b. 80¢
   c. 76¢
   d. NG

4.

   a. 4:25
   b. 3:25
   c. 5:15
   d. NG

5.

   a. 135
   b. 55
   c. 145
   d. NG

6.
   51
   + 37

   a. 14
   b. 98
   c. 89
   d. NG

7.
   29¢
   + 34¢

   a. 63¢
   b. 53¢
   c. 513
   d. NG

8.
   80
   + 70

   a. 160
   b. 150
   c. 10
   d. NG

9.
   76
   + 97

   a. 163
   b. 1,613
   c. 173
   d. NG

10.
    80
    − 30

    a. 50
    b. 110
    c. 40
    d. NG

11.
    59
    − 15

    a. 44
    b. 74
    c. 54
    d. NG

12.
    98¢
    − 35¢

    a. 133¢
    b. 36¢
    c. 63¢
    d. NG

13.
    71¢
    − 23¢

    a. 52¢
    b. 48¢
    c. 94¢
    d. NG

score

Adding and Subtracting 2-Digit Numbers

Lesson 9-1

Finding 2- or 3-Digit Sums

The Walkers planted 75 tomato plants and 49 pepper plants in their garden. How many plants are there in all?

We are looking for the total number of plants.

There are ____ tomato plants.

There are ____ pepper plants.

To find the total, we add ____ and ____.

Add the ones first. Regroup if needed.

$5 + 9 = 14$
$14 = 1$ ten and 4 ones

```
  1
  75
+ 49
-----
   4
```

Add the tens.

$1 + 7 + 4 = 12$
12 tens $= 1$ hundred and 2 tens

```
  1
  75
+ 49
-----
 124
```

There are ____ plants in all.

Getting Started

Add. Regroup if needed.

1. 68 + 79
2. 39 + 29
3. 65 + 25
4. 78 + 36
5. 47 + 41
6. 90 + 62
7. 57 + 37
8. 78 + 9
9. 87 + 78
10. 65 + 34
11. 46 + 27
12. 80 + 80

Lesson 9-1 • Finding 2- or 3-Digit Sums

Practice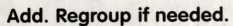

Add. Regroup if needed.

1. 11 + 46
2. 80 + 44
3. 49 + 6
4. 18 + 44
5. 99 + 33
6. 18 + 15

7. 36 + 64
8. 19 + 22
9. 23 + 39
10. 96 + 32
11. 8 + 48
12. 45 + 74

13. 79 + 89
14. 72 + 77
15. 27 + 17
16. 88 + 33
17. 28 + 45
18. 67 + 70

19. 49 + 9
20. 63 + 48
21. 48 + 86
22. 82 + 12
23. 67 + 23
24. 85 + 12

25. 56 + 84
26. 37 + 28
27. 44 + 37
28. 62 + 17
29. 59 + 98
30. 26 + 6

Problem Solving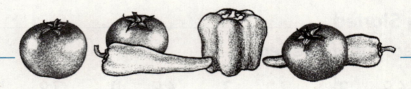

Solve.

31. Ellie picked 50 tomatoes in the morning and 80 in the afternoon. How many tomatoes did she pick?

    _____ tomatoes

32. Charley picked 75 green peppers and 65 yellow peppers. How many peppers did he pick?

    _____ peppers

Lesson 9-2

Column Addition

It's Algebra!

The students in Garden School sold cookies for charity. How many boxes of cookies did Holly, Keith, and Gloria sell altogether?

We want to know how many boxes of cookies Holly, Keith, and Gloria sold.

Holly sold _____ boxes.

Keith sold _____ boxes.

Gloria sold _____ boxes.

To find how many they sold altogether, we add _____, _____, and _____.

Boxes of Cookies SOLD

Holly	54 boxes
Jason	43 boxes
Keith	37 boxes
Gloria	21 boxes

Add the ones first. Regroup if needed.

$4 + 7 + 1 = 12$
$12 = 1$ ten and 2 ones

```
  1
  54
  37
+ 21
----
   2
```

Add the tens.

$1 + 5 + 3 + 2 = 11$
11 tens $= 1$ hundred and 1 ten

```
  1
  54
  37
+ 21
----
 112
```

They sold _____ boxes of cookies.

Getting Started

Add. Regroup if needed.

1. 16
    72
  + 35

2. 25
    54
  + 65

3. 41
    37
  + 96

4. 55
     8
  + 30

5. 14
    24
  + 36

6.   2
    86
  + 38

Lesson 9-2 • Column Addition

Practice

Add. Regroup if needed.

1. 23
   37
   + 90

2. 40
   30
   + 70

3.   6
   70
   + 58

4. 13
   33
   + 76

5. 11
   37
   + 59

6. 49
   10
   + 68

7. 10
   69
   + 18

8. 59
   61
   + 3

9. 51
   39
   + 97

10. 31
     6
    + 52

11. 10
    70
    + 80

12. 54
    34
    + 25

13. 86
     1
    + 8

14. 35
    30
    + 35

15. 83
     6
    + 54

16. 30
    19
    + 88

17. 82
    14
    + 18

18. 72
    23
    + 98

Now Try This!

If you toss a coin 30 times, how many times do you think it will land tails up?

_____ times

Try it.

Toss a coin 30 times.

How many heads did you get? _____

How many tails did you get? _____

Was your guess close? _____

158 one hundred fifty-eight

Lesson 9-2 • Column Addition

Name _____

Lesson 9-3

Subtracting With Regrouping

Greg sold 75 adult tickets to the school play. He sold 48 student tickets. How many more adult tickets did Greg sell?

We want to know how many more adult tickets were sold.

Greg sold _____ adult tickets.

He sold _____ student tickets.

To find how many more adult tickets were sold, we subtract _____ from _____.

REMEMBER Subtract the ones first.

Subtract the ones. Regroup if needed.	Subtract the tens.
$15 - 8 = 7$	$6 - 4 = 2$
$\begin{array}{r} ^{6}^{15} \\ \cancel{7}\cancel{5} \\ -48 \\ \hline 7 \end{array}$	$\begin{array}{r} ^{6}^{15} \\ \cancel{7}\cancel{5} \\ -48 \\ \hline 27 \end{array}$

Greg sold _____ more adult tickets.

Getting Started

Subtract. Regroup if needed.

1. 74
   − 26

2. 47
   − 33

3. 71
   − 51

4. 89
   − 76

5. 80
   − 52

6. 91
   − 27

Lesson 9-3 • Subtracting With Regrouping

one hundred fifty-nine **159**

Practice

Subtract. Regroup if needed.

1. 47 − 36
2. 66 − 34
3. 38 − 14
4. 75 − 68
5. 70 − 57
6. 61 − 44

7. 93 − 13
8. 32 − 15
9. 78 − 29
10. 61 − 28
11. 54 − 37
12. 63 − 29

13. 80 − 65
14. 52 − 30
15. 93 − 87
16. 17 − 11
17. 95 − 76
18. 75 − 59

19. 72 − 29
20. 87 − 42
21. 54 − 18
22. 31 − 29
23. 60 − 34
24. 82 − 20

25. 60 − 19
26. 55 − 23
27. 94 − 75
28. 27 − 20
29. 50 − 46
30. 37 − 11

Problem Solving

Solve.

31. Martin found 37 shells. He gave 18 shells to Nell. How many shells does Martin have left?

    _____ shells

32. Rona poured 65 cups of juice. She sold 28 cups. How many cups of juice were not sold?

    _____ cups of juice

Name _____

Lesson 9-4

Mixed Review

Add or subtract. Regroup if needed.

1. 35 + 23
2. 74 + 96
3. 90 + 57
4. 54 + 29
5. 58 + 36
6. 32 + 99

7. 49 − 15
8. 86 − 34
9. 90 − 25
10. 41 − 28
11. 72 − 33
12. 91 − 59

13. 63 + 33
14. 86 + 46
15. 57 − 50
16. 90 − 67
17. 75 + 95
18. 51 − 26

19. 53 + 24 + 87
20. 65 + 4 + 38
21. 40 + 21 + 30
22. 7 + 52 + 73
23. 32 + 14 + 94
24. 74 + 44 + 4

Solve.

25. There are 33 puppies in the pet store. There are 17 kittens. How many more puppies than kittens are there?

    _____ puppies

26. There are 75 goldfish and 85 guppies. How many fish are there altogether?

    _____ fish

27. There are 18 canaries and 26 parakeets. How many birds are there altogether?

    _____ birds

28. The pet store had 34 turtles. It sold 19. How many turtles were not sold?

    _____ turtles

Lesson 9-4 • Mixed Review

one hundred sixty-one **161**

Practice

Add or subtract. Regroup if needed.

1. 66 + 40
2. 97 + 41
3. 95 − 20
4. 91 − 59
5. 35 + 44
6. 79 + 44

7. 95 − 70
8. 73 − 26
9. 64 − 17
10. 79 + 74
11. 56 + 40
12. 69 + 64

13. 65 − 52
14. 95 + 74
15. 82 − 27
16. 77 − 49
17. 63 + 99
18. 95 − 74

Problem Solving

Solve.

19. Clown School has 61 happy clowns and 45 sad clowns. How many more happy clowns are there?

    _____ happy clowns

20. The circus needs 23 horses, 14 lions, and 18 dogs. How many animals does it need?

    _____ animals

21. 89 girls and 94 boys went to the circus. How many children went to the circus?

    _____ children

22. Jumbo, an elephant, is 53 years old. Atlas, an elephant, is 38 years old. How many years older is Jumbo?

    _____ years

Name _____

Lesson 9-5

Addition and Subtraction Sentences

Addition and subtraction problems are sometimes written as number sentences. If you cannot do the addition or subtraction in your head, copy the problem as shown below. Then you can add or subtract.

$23 + 42 =$ ___

$34 + 68 =$ __?__

Copy.
$$\begin{array}{r} 34 \\ +\ 68 \\ \hline \end{array}$$

Do.
$$\begin{array}{r} \overset{1}{3}4 \\ +\ 68 \\ \hline 102 \end{array}$$

Write the answer on the line.
$34 + 68 =$ ____

$93 - 77 =$ __?__

Copy.
$$\begin{array}{r} 93 \\ -\ 77 \\ \hline \end{array}$$

Do.
$$\begin{array}{r} {}^{8}\cancel{9}{}^{13}\cancel{3} \\ -\ 77 \\ \hline 16 \end{array}$$

Write the answer on the line.
$93 - 77 =$ ____

Getting Started

Copy and add. Write the answer on the line.

1. $79 + 57 =$ ____

2. $47 + 12 + 96 =$ ____

Lesson 9-5 • Addition and Subtraction Sentences   one hundred sixty-three **163**

Practice

Copy and do. Write the answer on the line.

1. 38 − 13 = ____
2. 80 − 5 = ____
3. 63 − 7 = ____
4. 62 + 14 = ____
5. 23 + 4 + 32 = ____
6. 99 + 99 = ____

Now Try This!

Complete each table.

Add 5.	
37	
22	
43	
55	

Add 7.	
21	
52	
43	
67	

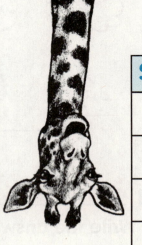

Subtract 4.	
41	
35	
60	
23	

Lesson 9-6

Subtracting Money

Mel had 85¢.
He bought a balloon.
How much does he have left?

We want to find out how much money Mel has left.

Mel had ____.

The balloon cost ____.

To find out how much money Mel has left, we subtract ____ from ____.

Subtract the pennies first.	Subtract the dimes.
7 15 8̸5̸¢ − 2 9¢ ────── 6¢	7 15 8̸5̸¢ − 2 9¢ ────── 5 6¢

Mel has ____ left.

Getting Started

Subtract.

1. 48¢ − 21¢
2. 73¢ − 32¢
3. 95¢ − 70¢
4. 74¢ − 19¢
5. 91¢ − 68¢
6. 64¢ − 44¢

Find out how much is left.

	You had	You bought	How much is left?
7.	75¢	62¢	
8.	83¢	58¢	

Lesson 9-6 • Subtracting Money

Practice

Subtract.

1. 90¢ − 30¢
2. 50¢ − 36¢
3. 87¢ − 82¢
4. 33¢ − 9¢
5. 96¢ − 49¢
6. 70¢ − 17¢

7. 61¢ − 24¢
8. 93¢ − 78¢
9. 62¢ − 6¢
10. 28¢ − 16¢
11. 74¢ − 39¢
12. 44¢ − 18¢

Find out how much is left.

	You had	You bought	How much is left?
13.	75¢	18¢	
14.	88¢	45¢	
15.	67¢	38¢	
16.	50¢	18¢	
17.	91¢	55¢	

Lesson 9-7

Adding Money

Bear and Lion are putting their money together to buy a game. How much money do they have altogether?

We want to know how much money they have altogether.

Bear has ____.

Lion has ____.

To find how much they have altogether, we add ____ and ____.

Add the pennies first.	Add the dimes.
$\begin{array}{r} {\scriptstyle 1} \\ 57¢ \\ +95¢ \\ \hline 2¢ \end{array}$	$\begin{array}{r} {\scriptstyle 1} \\ 57¢ \\ +95¢ \\ \hline 152¢ \end{array}$

152¢ = $1.52

Bear and Lion have _____.

Getting Started

Add. Then write each answer in dollar notation.

1. 15¢
  + 85¢

2. 63¢
  + 25¢

3. 57¢
    32¢
  + 57¢

4. 25¢
    3¢
  + 75¢

5. 58¢
    20¢
  + 49¢

Lesson 9-7 • Adding Money   one hundred sixty-seven **167**

Practice

Add. Then write each answer in dollar notation.

1. 75¢ + 52¢
2. 98¢ + 95¢
3. 61¢ + 89¢
4. 50¢ + 41¢
5. 83¢ + 42¢

6. 92¢ + 69¢
7. 88¢ + 63¢
8. 12¢ + 98¢
9. 55¢ + 45¢
10. 77¢ + 37¢

11. 87¢ + 62¢
12. 56¢ + 39¢
13. 86¢ + 3¢ + 46¢
14. 14¢ + 34¢ + 26¢
15. 55¢ + 11¢ + 45¢

Problem Solving

Write each answer.

16. Who has the most money? _____

17. Who has the least money? _____

18. How much money do Craig and José have together? _____

19. How much more money does José have than Craig? _____

☆ Lana has $1.25.
☆ Craig has 37¢.
☆ José has 75¢.

168 one hundred sixty-eight

Lesson 9-7 • Adding Money

Name _____

Lesson 9-8

Estimating Sums

It's Algebra!

Sherri has $2.00. She wants to buy the doll and the softball. She does not know if she has enough money. She can estimate by rounding each item to the nearest ten cents to find out.

If the digit in the pennies place is 5 or greater, round up to the nearest ten cents.

If the digit in the pennies place is less than 5, round down to the nearest ten cents.

The cost of the softball is _____.

The cost of the doll is _____.

Round to the nearest 10 cents.		Estimate.

```
  91¢  →   90¢           90¢
+ 65¢  → + 70¢         + 70¢
                         160¢   (160¢ = $1.60)
```

The estimate is $1.60. Sherri has enough money to buy the doll and the softball.

Getting Started

Estimate. Show how you rounded.

1. Mick has 87¢. Melissa has 75¢. About how much money do they have in all?

    _____

2. Jamal has 68¢. Nadine has 88¢. About how much money do they have in all?

    _____

3. Elise spent 42¢ to buy a pencil. She spent 53¢ to buy a pen. About how much did Elise spend in all?

    _____

4. Suzie has 52¢ saved. Her mother gives her 75¢. About how much money does Suzie have now?

    _____

Practice

Estimate. Show how you rounded.

1. 28¢
 + 27¢

2. 52¢
 + 83¢

3. 62¢
 + 47¢

4. 39¢
 + 26¢

Problem Solving

5. Jenny bought a birthday card for 83¢. She also bought a pin for 92¢. About how much did Jenny spend altogether?

   _____

6. Max donated 38¢ to his sister's school band. He also donated 51¢ to the dog pound. About how much did Max donate in all?

   _____

7. Ted bought a baseball for 93¢. He also bought a baseball cap for 95¢. About how much did Ted spend altogether?

   _____

8. Laura saved 49¢. Her grandmother gave her 47¢. About how much money does Laura have?

   _____

Now Try This!

What money amounts round to 70¢ when rounded to the nearest ten cents?

_____

_____

Problem Solving: Choose an Operation

Decide if you need to add or subtract. Then solve.

1. Melissa has 75¢. She bought a beach ball. How much does she have left?

   _____
   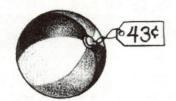

2. How much did Yong pay for both toys?

   _____

3. Circle the toy that costs more. How much more does it cost?

   _____

4. Ashley bought a yo-yo. She gave the clerk 50¢. How much change did she get?

   _____
   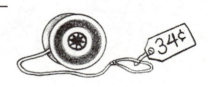

5. Steven had 95¢. He bought a top. How much does he have left?

   _____

6. Mr. Jon took his daughter to a movie. How much did he spend for the tickets?

   _____

7. What is the cost of a bat and a ball together?

   _____

8. Kiku and Cathy each bought a glove. How much did they pay altogether?

   _____

Practice

Decide if you need to add or subtract. Then solve.

1. How much more did Cary pay for the teddy bear?

   _____

2. How much did Dino pay for the scissors and crayons?

   _____

   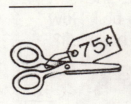 

3. How much did Al pay for the hammer and pliers?

   _____

4. Kasey had 85¢. She bought a top. How much does she have left?

   _____

5. How much more did Rhea pay for the truck?

   _____

6. What is the cost for all three items?

   _____

7. How much did Bart pay for all three toys?

   _____

8. How much do the three toys cost altogether?

   _____

Lesson 9-9 • Problem Solving: Choose an Operation

Name _____

Chapter 9 Test

Add or subtract.

1. 38
   +19

2. 46
   +21

3. 15
   +83

4. 24
   +63

5. 25
   +38

6. 46
   +26

7. 87
   +62

8. 32
   +77

9. 77
   +43

10. 69
   +66

11. 83
   +58

12. 67
   +63

13. 86
   −23

14. 75
   −14

15. 67
   −17

16. 93
   −24

17. 51
   −39

18. 75
   −48

19. 23
    14
   +42

20. 10
    50
   +70

21. 13
    65
   +63

22. 43
    73
   + 6

23. 45
    50
   +55

24. 32
    27
   +93

25. 34
    21
   +22

26. 53
    72
   + 8

27. 32
    42
   +26

28. 20
    60
   +40

29. 40
    51
   +69

30. 16
    75
   +60

Add or subtract. Then write each answer in dollar notation.

31. 35¢
   +75¢

32. 57¢
   +98¢

33. 97¢
   −65¢

34. 75¢
   +50¢

35. 83¢
   −25¢

_____   _____   _____   _____   _____

Chapter 9 • Test

Cumulative Assessment

Circle the letter of the correct answer.

1. 7 + 6
   a. 12
   b. 13
   c. 14
   d. NG

2. 8 + 9 =
   a. 17
   b. 16
   c. 18
   d. NG

3. 12 − 5
   a. 17
   b. 15
   c. 7
   d. NG

4. 15 − 6 =
   a. 8
   b. 21
   c. 11
   d. NG

5.
   a. 76
   b. 57
   c. 67
   d. NG

6. 39 41
   a. >
   b. <

7. 69 + 89
   a. 158
   b. 20
   c. 148
   d. NG

8. 25 + 34 + 17
   a. 66
   b. 77
   c. 76
   d. NG

9. 78 − 45
   a. 123
   b. 33
   c. 113
   d. NG

10. 91 − 25
    a. 66
    b. 74
    c. 76
    d. NG

11. 48 + 35 =
    a. 82
    b. 83
    c. 73
    d. NG

12. 57 + 6
    a. 51
    b. 53
    c. 63
    d. NG

13. 71 − 29 =
    a. 58
    b. 42
    c. 52
    d. NG

score

Name _____

Adding 3-Digit Numbers

Chapter 10

Lesson 10-1

Place Value Through 1,000

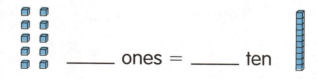
____ ones = ____ ten

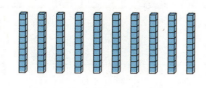
____ tens = ____ hundred

____ hundreds = ____ thousand

Count by tens. Write the missing numbers.

  10   20   ____ ____ ____ ____ ____ ____ ____ ____

Count by hundreds. Write the missing numbers.

  100   200 ____ ____ ____ ____ ____ ____ ____ ____

Getting Started

How many hundreds, tens, and ones are there? Write the numbers.

____ hundreds ____ tens ____ ones
____

Lesson 10-1 • Place Value Through 1,000   one hundred seventy-five **175**

Practice

Write how many hundreds, tens, and ones there are. Write each number.

1.

   ____ hundred ____ tens ____ ones

   ____

2.

   ____ hundreds ____ tens ____ ones

   ____

3.

   ____ hundreds ____ tens ____ ones

   ____

4.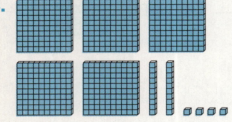

   ____ hundreds ____ tens ____ ones

   ____

5.

   ____ hundreds ____ tens ____ ones

   ____

6.

   ____ hundred ____ tens ____ ones

   ____

7.

   ____ hundreds ____ ten ____ ones

   ____

Lesson 10-1 • Place Value Through 1,000

Name _____

Lesson 10-2

Review Adding 2-Digit Numbers

The hardware store had a sale.
How many tools were for sale?

We want to know the number of tools for sale.

The store had ____ hammers.

It had ____ saws.

To find how many tools were for sale, we add ____ and ____.

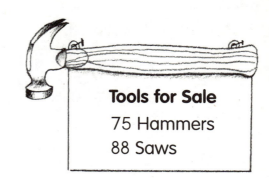

Tools for Sale
75 Hammers
88 Saws

Add the ones first. Regroup if needed.	Add the tens.

```
   1              1
   75            75
 + 88          + 88
 ─────        ─────
    3          163
```

The store had ____ tools for sale.

Getting Started

Add. Regroup if needed.

1. 37   2. 96   3. 39   4. 81   5. 27
  + 82   + 44   + 99   + 85   + 73

6. 14   7. 75   8. 49   9. 52   10. 63
  + 96   + 50   + 98   + 77   + 58

Lesson 10-2 • Review Adding 2-Digit Numbers   one hundred seventy-seven **177**

Practice

Add. Regroup if needed.

1. 42 + 83
2. 95 + 70
3. 84 + 29
4. 39 + 57
5. 79 + 83
6. 18 + 67

7. 68 + 54
8. 86 + 76
9. 22 + 54
10. 82 + 68
11. 56 + 55
12. 90 + 53

13. 63 + 82
14. 97 + 85
15. 78 + 79
16. 51 + 84
17. 68 + 24
18. 77 + 89

Now Try This!

Solve.

1. Add two numbers. The sum is 96. One number is 35. What is the other number?

   _____

2. Subtract two numbers. The answer is 38. The larger number is 96. What is the other number?

   _____

3. Add two numbers. The sum is 91. One number is 36. What is the other number?

   _____

4. Subtract two numbers. The answer is 57. The smaller number is 19. What is the larger number?

   _____

Name _____

Lesson 10-3

Adding a 3-Digit and a 1-Digit Number

Some students and parents from Allen School went to Clown School. How many people studied clowning?

We want to know how many went to Clown School.

There were ____ students and ____ parents attending Clown School.

To find how many people were attending, we add ____ and ____.

Add the ones first. Regroup if needed.	Add the tens.	Add the hundreds.

```
   1              1              1
  154            154            154
+   8          +   8          +   8
─────          ─────          ─────
    2             62            162
```

There were ____ people attending Clown School.

Getting Started

Add. Regroup if needed.

1. 237   2. 374   3. 964   4. 555   5. 423
  +   5   +   7   +   6   +   5   +   9
  ─────   ─────   ─────   ─────   ─────

6. 105   7. 675   8. 815   9. 276   10. 349
  +   8   +   6   +   7   +   2   +   8
  ─────   ─────   ─────   ─────   ─────

Lesson 10-3 • Adding a 3-Digit and a 1-Digit Number   one hundred seventy-nine **179**

Practice

Add. Regroup if needed.

1. 774 + 9
2. 588 + 2
3. 517 + 9
4. 603 + 7
5. 357 + 4

6. 282 + 7
7. 156 + 6
8. 921 + 8
9. 813 + 9
10. 628 + 5

11. 487 + 4
12. 307 + 5
13. 156 + 6
14. 385 + 3
15. 906 + 8

16. 9 + 286
17. 986 + 6
18. 9 + 849
19. 383 + 8
20. 566 + 7

Problem Solving

Solve.

21. There were 335 circus tickets sold. Then 6 more tickets were sold. How many tickets were sold?

    _____ tickets

22. Pat sold 248 bags of popcorn at the circus. Then he sold 7 more bags. How many bags of popcorn did Pat sell?

    _____ bags

Lesson 10-4

Adding a 3-Digit and a 2-Digit Number

Both students and parents bought tickets to the school carnival. How many tickets were sold?

There were _____ student tickets sold.

There were _____ adult tickets sold.

To find how many tickets were sold, we add _____ and _____.

I sold 257 student tickets.

I sold 82 adult tickets.

Add the ones first. Regroup if needed.	Add the tens. Regroup if needed.	Add the hundreds.
7 + 2 = 9 ones No trade is needed.	5 + 8 = 13 tens 13 tens = 1 hundred and 3 tens	1 + 2 = 3 hundreds
257 + 82 ——— 9	1 257 + 82 ——— 39	1 257 + 82 ——— 339

There were _____ carnival tickets sold.

Getting Started

Add. Regroup if needed.

1. 580 + 87
2. 317 + 51
3. 271 + 46
4. 450 + 92
5. 694 + 32
6. 474 + 21
7. 425 + 84
8. 132 + 59
9. 230 + 87
10. 488 + 70

Lesson 10-4 • Adding a 3-Digit and a 2-Digit Number

Practice

Add. Regroup if needed.

1. 279 + 12
2. 478 + 14
3. 265 + 23
4. 343 + 49
5. 279 + 80

6. 189 + 80
7. 191 + 53
8. 149 + 20
9. 367 + 51
10. 186 + 21

11. 234 + 75
12. 339 + 53
13. 322 + 74
14. 407 + 54
15. 803 + 27

16. 725 + 15
17. 457 + 92
18. 559 + 24
19. 753 + 38
20. 442 + 93

Problem Solving

Solve.

21. Erin had 276 marbles. Devin gave her 70 more marbles. How many marbles does Erin have now?

    _____ marbles

22. Jason saved 358 stamps. His sister gave him 27 more stamps. How many stamps does Jason have now?

    _____ stamps

Lesson 10-5

Adding With 2 Regroupings

The school bookstore has 275 red pencils and 86 blue pencils. How many pencils does it have?

We are looking for the total number of pencils.

There are _____ red pencils and _____ blue pencils.

To find the total number of pencils, we add _____ and _____.

Add the ones first. Regroup if needed.	Add the tens. Regroup if needed.	Add the hundreds.
5 + 6 = 11 ones 11 ones = 1 ten and 1 one	1 + 7 + 8 = 16 tens 16 tens = 1 hundred and 6 tens	1 + 2 = 3 hundreds
1 275 + 86 ――― 1	1 1 275 + 86 ――― 61	1 1 275 + 86 ――― 361

The school book store has _____ pencils.

Getting Started

Add. Regroup if needed.

1. 326
    + 79

2. 542
    + 88

3. 384
    + 16

4. 794
    + 59

5. 453
    + 98

6. 919
    + 67

7.   68
    +496

8. 154
    + 96

9. 643
    + 46

10. 643
    + 57

one hundred eighty-three **183**

Practice

Add. Regroup if needed.

1. 264 + 53
2. 486 + 45
3. 332 + 79
4. 517 + 98
5. 726 + 75

6. 154 + 95
7. 781 + 38
8. 857 + 69
9. 695 + 98
10. 201 + 99

11. 386 + 76
12. 850 + 92
13. 468 + 73
14. 729 + 58
15. 596 + 65

16. 271 + 27
17. 621 + 84
18. 586 + 76
19. 901 + 65
20. 153 + 73

21. 615 + 85
22. 723 + 68
23. 265 + 39
24. 37 + 685
25. 89 + 527

Now Try This!

Complete each Magic Square.

		6
3	5	7
	9	

	0	
2	4	6
	8	1

9	2	7
	10	3

184 one hundred eighty-four

Lesson 10-5 • Adding With 2 Regroupings

Lesson 10-6

Practice Adding With 1 or 2 Regroupings

There were 355 books and 97 tapes checked out of the school library last week. How many books and tapes were checked out altogether?

We want to know how many items were checked out.

There were _____ books and _____ tapes.

To find out how many were checked out altogether, we add _____ and _____.

Add the ones first. Regroup if needed.

```
  1
  355
+  97
-----
    2
```

Add the tens. Regroup if needed.

```
 1 1
  355
+  97
-----
   52
```

Add the hundreds.

```
 1 1
  355
+  97
-----
  452
```

There were _____ books and tapes checked out of the library.

Getting Started

Add. Regroup if needed.

1. 347 + 46
2. 275 + 82
3. 586 + 97
4. 164 + 76
5. 795 + 55

6. 429 + 71
7. 650 + 60
8. 931 + 57
9. 219 + 99
10. 352 + 68

Lesson 10-6 • Practice Adding With 1 or 2 Regroupings one hundred eighty-five **185**

Practice

Add. Regroup if needed.

1. 127 + 31
2. 275 + 18
3. 756 + 87
4. 635 + 87
5. 362 + 89
6. 475 + 75
7. 599 + 99
8. 938 + 25
9. 484 + 16
10. 95 + 127

Now Try This!

Color each block blue. Then write your answer on the line.

1. 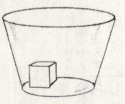 If I want to have an equal chance of drawing a red or blue, I would put in _____ red block(s).

2. 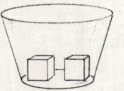 If I want blue to be more likely than red, I would put in _____ red block(s).

3. 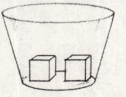 If I want blue to be less likely than red, I would put in _____ red blocks.

4. 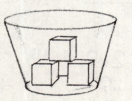 If I want an equal chance of drawing a red or blue, I would put in _____ red blocks.

Name _____

Lesson 10-7

Adding Two 3-Digit Numbers

Plans were made by 128 parents of Lincoln School for a spring picnic. 375 children signed up to go. How many children and parents went to the picnic?

We want to know how many were at the picnic.

There were _____ children at the picnic.

There were _____ parents.

To find how many people were at the picnic, we add _____ and _____.

Add the ones first. Regroup if needed.	Add the tens. Regroup if needed.	Add the hundreds.
1 375 +128 ——— 3	1 1 375 +128 ——— 03	1 1 375 +128 ——— 503

There were _____ people at the picnic.

Getting Started

Add. Regroup if needed.

1. 341 + 237
2. 655 + 329
3. 752 + 198
4. 437 + 463
5. 586 + 145

6. 176 + 532
7. 595 + 187
8. 215 + 675
9. 753 + 189
10. 375 + 275

Lesson 10-7 • Adding Two 3-Digit Numbers   one hundred eighty-seven **187**

Practice

Add. Regroup if needed.

1. 128 + 239
2. 243 + 266
3. 154 + 186
4. 475 + 140
5. 500 + 250

6. 469 + 241
7. 428 + 395
8. 165 + 378
9. 752 + 108
10. 394 + 237

11. 417 + 230
12. 466 + 427
13. 352 + 248
14. 273 + 468
15. 116 + 599

Problem Solving

Solve.

16. The people at the spring picnic used 278 hot dog buns and 385 hamburger buns. How many buns were used?

    _____ buns

17. 325 cups of orange juice and 375 cups of milk were served. How many cups were served?

    _____ cups

18. 158 people swam and 263 rowed boats. How many people were swimming or rowing boats?

    _____ people

19. 185 children and 77 adults played bingo at the picnic. How many people played bingo?

    _____ people

188 one hundred eighty-eight

Lesson 10-7 • Adding Two 3-Digit Numbers

Name _____

Lesson 10-8

Adding 3-Digit Numbers

Roger's grandfather works in a bakery. Each day he bakes 228 loaves of white bread and 198 loaves of wheat bread. How many loaves does he bake each day?

We want to know how many loaves he bakes each day.

He bakes ____ loaves of white bread and ____ loaves of wheat bread each day.

To find the total number of loaves, we add ____ and ____.

Add the ones first. Regroup if needed.	Add the tens. Regroup if needed.	Add the hundreds.
$^{1}$ 228 $+198$ ――― 6	$^{1\,1}$ 228 $+198$ ――― 26	$^{1\,1}$ 228 $+198$ ――― 426

Roger's grandfather bakes ____ loaves of bread each day.

Getting Started

Add. Regroup if needed.

1. 357 + 548 = ____

2. 269 + 85 = ____

3. 296
 + 313

4. 158
 + 675

5. 391
 + 193

6. 748
 + 177

7. 624
 + 257

Lesson 10-8 • Adding 3-Digit Numbers

Practice

Add. Regroup if needed.

1. 166 + 351 = _____

2. 449 + 276 = _____

3. 256 + 68 = _____

4. 159 + 681 = _____

5. 275
  + 323

6. 384
  + 119

7. 525
  + 195

8. 436
  + 297

9. 523
  + 288

10. 35
   + 265

11. 96
   + 875

12. 105
   + 196

13. 57
   + 288

14. 441
   + 82

15. 73
   + 580

16. 394
   + 262

17. 546
   + 254

18. 9
   + 215

19. 751
   + 163

20. 95
   + 438

21. 526
   + 175

22. 253
   + 288

23. 615
   + 173

24. 252
   + 308

190 one hundred ninety   Lesson 10-8 • Adding 3-Digit Numbers

Name _____

Lesson 10-9

Adding Money

Dino went to the store for his mother. How much did he spend for bread and meat?

We want to know how much money he spent.

The bread cost _____.

The meat cost _____.

To find the cost of the bread and the meat, we add _____ and _____.

Add the pennies first. Regroup if needed.	Add the dimes. Regroup if needed.	Add the dollars. Regroup if needed.	Put in the dollar sign.
$\overset{1}{}$ $\$1.2\textcolor{blue}{8}$ $+2.9\textcolor{blue}{5}$ ——— $\textcolor{blue}{3}$	$\overset{1}{}\overset{1}{}$ $\$1.\textcolor{blue}{2}8$ $+2.\textcolor{blue}{9}5$ ——— $\textcolor{blue}{2}3$	$\overset{1}{}\overset{1}{}$ $\$\textcolor{blue}{1}.28$ $+\textcolor{blue}{2}.95$ ——— $\textcolor{blue}{4}23$	$\overset{1}{}\overset{1}{}$ $\$1.28$ $+2.95$ ——— $\textcolor{blue}{\$}4.23$

Dino spent _____ in all.

Getting Started

Add. Regroup if needed.

1. $\$1.25$
    $+3.74$

2. $\$2.19$
    $+4.66$

3. $\$5.75$
    $+2.75$

4. $\$4.89$
    $+3.69$

5. $\$5.57$
    $+3.28$

6. $\$0.49$
    $+6.49$

7. $\$3.25$
    $+2.98$

8. $\$6.19$
    $+1.65$

9. $\$7.08$
    $+1.98$

10. $\$2.34$
    $+3.66$

Practice

Add. Regroup if needed.

1. $4.38 + 1.28
2. $3.15 + 3.42
3. $4.87 + 3.76
4. $2.65 + 0.65
5. $7.09 + 1.95

Problem Solving

Add to find the total cost.

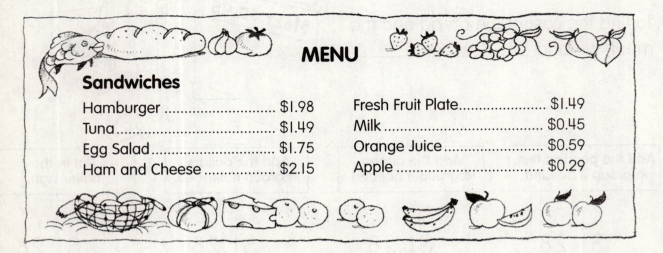

MENU

Sandwiches
- Hamburger $1.98
- Tuna $1.49
- Egg Salad $1.75
- Ham and Cheese $2.15

- Fresh Fruit Plate $1.49
- Milk $0.45
- Orange Juice $0.59
- Apple $0.29

6. Hamburger
   Milk

7. Fresh Fruit Plate
   Milk

8. Tuna Sandwich
   Orange Juice

9. Ham and Cheese Sandwich
   Apple

10. Hamburger
    Fresh Fruit Plate

11. Tuna Sandwich
    Fresh Fruit Plate

12. Egg Salad Sandwich
    Milk

13. Ham and Cheese Sandwich
    Orange Juice

Name _____

Lesson 10-10

Estimating Cost

It's Algebra!

Stephanie wants to buy the T-shirt and the pair of pants. She wants to know about how much she will have to pay. Stephanie can round to the nearest dollar.

If the digit in the dimes place is 5 or greater, round up.

If the digit in the dimes place is less than 5, round down.

The cost of the T-shirt is $3.85

The cost of the pair of pants is _____.

Round to the nearest dollar.

$ 3.85 → $ 4.00 round up
+ 4.22 → + 4.00 round down

Estimate.

$ 4.00
+ 4.00

$ 8.00

Stephanie will spend about _____ to buy the T-shirt and pants.

Getting Started

Estimate. Show how you rounded.

1. Kathy has $5.26. Donna has $3.19. About how much money do they have in all?

2. Marcus earned $5.45 for delivering newspapers. He earned $3.82 for walking his neighbor's dog. About how much money did Marcus earn altogether?

3. Mrs. Wilkins spent $3.79 on orange juice and $4.92 on milk. About how much did Mrs. Wilkins spend altogether?

4. Samantha bought a skirt for $6.25. She bought a matching top for $2.45. About how much did Samantha spend in all?

Practice

Estimate. Show how you rounded.

1. $5.87
 + 2.08

2. $4.29
 + 4.88

3. $3.64
 + 5.46

4. $6.31
 + 1.87

Problem Solving

5. Rosie has $3.83 in her purse. Her grandmother gave her $4.25. About how much money does Rosie have now?

   _____

6. Artie has $1.83 in pennies and $4.20 in nickels in his piggy bank. About how much money does Artie have altogether?

   _____

Now Try This!

1. What is the greatest amount of money that rounds to $5.00 when rounded to the nearest dollar?

   _____

2. What is the least amount of money that rounds to $5.00 when rounded to the nearest dollar?

   _____

Name _____

Problem Solving Lesson 10-11

Problem Solving: Use Information From a List

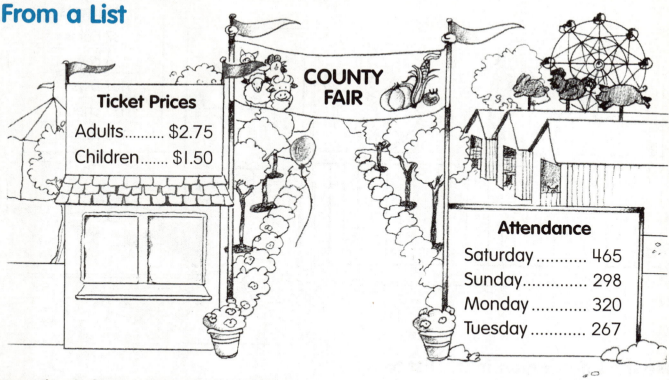

Ticket Prices
Adults $2.75
Children $1.50

Attendance
Saturday 465
Sunday 298
Monday 320
Tuesday 267

Use the information in the lists to solve each problem.

1. Mr. Brooks took his 8-year-old daughter to the county fair. How much did he pay for two tickets?

   _____

2. Mr. and Mrs. Velez went to the fair. How much did they pay for two adult tickets?

   _____

3. Robin and Peter went to the fair. How much did they pay for two children's tickets?

   _____

4. How many people went to the fair on Sunday and Monday?

   _____

5. If Robin and Peter in Exercise 3 had $5.00, could they have bought one more child's ticket?

   _____

6. Were there more people at the fair on Saturday and Sunday or Monday and Tuesday?

   _____

Lesson 10-11 • Problem Solving: Use Information From a List   one hundred ninety-five **195**

Practice

County Fair Animals
87 horses
256 cows
107 pigs
127 sheep
148 rabbits

Use the information in the list to solve each problem.

1. How many horses and cows were shown at the fair?

   _____ horses and cows

2. How many sheep and rabbits were shown at the fair?

   _____ sheep and rabbits

3. How many horses and rabbits were shown at the fair?

   _____ horses and rabbits

4. How many pigs and sheep were shown at the fair?

   _____ pigs and sheep

5. How many pigs and rabbits were shown at the fair?

   _____ pigs and rabbits

6. How many cows and sheep were shown at the fair?

   _____ cows and sheep

Chapter 10 Test

Name _____

Add. Regroup if needed.

1. 341 + 7
2. 188 + 6
3. 259 + 4
4. 525 + 5
5. 707 + 9

6. 218 + 81
7. 175 + 16
8. 387 + 57
9. 696 + 73
10. 575 + 25

11. 27 + 365
12. 56 + 128
13. 75 + 250
14. 126 + 109
15. 361 + 278

16. 613 + 274
17. 338 + 255
18. 459 + 382
19. 175 + 328
20. 524 + 176

21. $2.25 + 0.31
22. $3.36 + 1.47
23. $5.23 + 1.95
24. $3.37 + 5.63

Solve.

25. Jaime spent $2.75. Mona spent $3.65. How much did they spend altogether?

    _____

26. The Browns drove 245 miles on Saturday. They drove 188 miles on Sunday. How many miles did they drive altogether?

    _____ miles

Cumulative Assessment

Circle the letter of the correct answer.

1.
   a. 1:25
   b. 2:25
   c. 3:25
   d. NG

2.
   a. 36
   b. 64
   c. 46
   d. NG

3.
   a. 204
   b. 240
   c. 402
   d. NG

4. 38 ◯ 52
   a. >
   b. <

5.
   a. $1.66
   b. 60¢
   c. $1.56
   d. NG

6. 98
   − 26
   a. 124
   b. 72
   c. 36
   d. NG

7. 84
   − 47
   a. 47
   b. 131
   c. 43
   d. NG

8. 91
   − 27
   a. 74
   b. 64
   c. 76
   d. NG

9. 38 + 99 =
   a. 127
   b. 1217
   c. 137
   d. NG

10. 75
    + 85
    a. 150
    b. 170
    c. 160
    d. NG

11. 346
    + 73
    a. 319
    b. 419
    c. 429
    d. NG

12. 638
    + 267
    a. 905
    b. 895
    c. 805
    d. NG

13. 135
    + 396
    a. 421
    b. 531
    c. 431
    d. NG

score

Subtracting 3-Digit Numbers

Chapter 11

Lesson 11-1

Subtracting a 1-Digit From a 2-Digit Number

The Tidy Pet Shop had 33 finches. A total of 8 finches were sold. How many are left?

We are looking for the number not sold.

The pet shop had ____ finches.

It sold ____ finches.

To find how many are left, we subtract ____ from ____.

Subtract the ones. Regroup if needed.	Subtract the tens.

2 13
3̸3̸
− 8
―――
    5
	2 13
	3̸3̸
	− 8
	―――
	  25

There are ____ finches left.

Getting Started

Subtract. Regroup if needed.

1. 37   2. 49   3. 32   4. 58   5. 65
   − 5   − 7   − 6   − 9   − 7
   ―――   ―――   ―――   ―――   ―――

Lesson 11-1 • Subtracting a 1-Digit From a 2-Digit Number

Practice

Subtract. Regroup if needed.

1. 18
   − 5

2. 27
   − 3

3. 13
   − 4

4. 57
   − 6

5. 41
   − 8

6. 63
   − 6

7. 45
   − 2

8. 77
   − 8

9. 88
   − 6

10. 93
    − 4

11. 25
    − 5

12. 38
    − 1

13. 57
    − 9

14. 47
    − 3

15. 63
    − 7

16. 31
    − 7

17. 87
    − 8

18. 68
    − 3

19. 44
    − 8

20. 55
    − 7

Problem Solving

Solve.

21. The pet shop had 42 kittens for sale. It sold 9 kittens. How many kittens are left?

    _____ kittens

22. The pet shop has 61 dog collars for sale. Sal sold 7 collars. How many collars are left?

    _____ collars

23. There were 55 fish. Trish bought 9. How many fish are left?

    _____ fish

24. There were 75 puppies for sale. Walter sold 6. How many puppies are left?

    _____ puppies

Name _____ **Lesson 11-2**

Subtracting 2-Digit Numbers

Dana School had a roller skating party. There were 65 children and 27 adults skating. How many more children than adults were skating?

We want to know how many more children than adults were skating.

There were _____ children and _____ adults at the skating party.

To find how many more children than adults were skating, we subtract _____ from _____.

Subtract the ones. Regroup if needed.	Subtract the tens.
5 15 6̸5̸ − 27 ───── 8	5 15 6̸5̸ − 27 ───── 3 8

There are _____ more children than adults skating.

Getting Started

Subtract. Regroup if needed.

1. 78 − 25	2. 96 − 71	3. 86 − 48	4. 51 − 22	5. 83 − 66

Lesson 11-2 • Subtracting 2-Digit Numbers two hundred one **201**

Practice

Subtract. Regroup if needed.

1. 47 − 41
2. 67 − 17
3. 92 − 60
4. 96 − 89
5. 63 − 59

6. 73 − 26
7. 61 − 45
8. 96 − 78
9. 81 − 43
10. 65 − 47

11. 95 − 87
12. 88 − 83
13. 92 − 63
14. 49 − 25
15. 38 − 16

16. 62 − 14
17. 71 − 31
18. 66 − 49
19. 87 − 36
20. 64 − 16

21. 72 − 43
22. 52 − 30
23. 47 − 21
24. 63 − 39
25. 81 − 56

Problem Solving

Solve.

26. There were 41 girls and 24 boys skating. How many more girls than boys were skating?

    _____ more girls

27. Art skated around the rink 75 times. Ro skated around the rink 57 times. How many more times did Art skate around the rink?

    _____ times

Subtracting a 1-Digit From a 3-Digit Number

341 children went to the zoo.
9 parents went to the zoo.
How many more children
than parents went to the zoo?

We want to know how many more children than parents went to the zoo.

There are _____ children.

There are _____ parents.

To find how many more children went, we subtract _____ from _____.

Subtract the ones. Regroup if needed.	Subtract the tens.	Subtract the hundreds.
$\begin{array}{r} 3\,11 \\ 3\cancel{4}\cancel{1} \\ -9 \\ \hline 2 \end{array}$	$\begin{array}{r} 3\,11 \\ 3\cancel{4}\cancel{1} \\ -9 \\ \hline 32 \end{array}$	$\begin{array}{r} 3\,11 \\ \cancel{3}\cancel{4}\cancel{1} \\ -9 \\ \hline 332 \end{array}$

There are _____ more children than parents.

Getting Started

Subtract. Regroup if needed.

1. 127
  −   5
  ___

2. 252
  −   8
  ___

3. 512
  −   9
  ___

4. 331
  −   6
  ___

5. 747
  −   6
  ___

Lesson 11-3 • Subtracting a 1-Digit From a 3-Digit Number

Practice

Subtract. Regroup if needed.

1. 229 − 4
2. 636 − 8
3. 399 − 9
4. 851 − 7
5. 233 − 4

6. 137 − 5
7. 141 − 7
8. 725 − 6
9. 911 − 3
10. 673 − 5

11. 252 − 6
12. 341 − 9
13. 585 − 7
14. 463 − 9
15. 224 − 6

Now Try This!

1.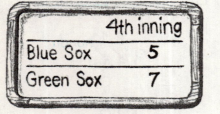

   Final Score: 9 to 6

   Which team won? _____

   How do you know?

   _____
   _____
   _____
   _____

2.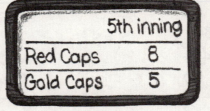

   Final Score: 8 to 7

   Which team won? _____

   How do you know?

   _____
   _____
   _____
   _____

Name _____

Lesson 11-4

Subtracting Multiples of 10

Morgan's Used Cars sold 256 cars in June and 80 cars in July. How many more cars were sold in June?

We want to know how many more cars were sold in June.

There were _____ cars sold in June and _____ cars sold in July.

To find how many more cars were sold in June, we subtract _____ from _____.

Subtract the ones. Regroup if needed.	Subtract the tens. Regroup if needed.	Subtract the hundreds.
6 − 0 = 6 ones	15 − 8 = 7 tens	1 − 0 = 1 hundred
256 − 80 ‾‾‾‾ 6	1 15 2̸5̸6 − 80 ‾‾‾‾ 76	1 15 2̸5̸6 − 80 ‾‾‾‾ 176

There were _____ more cars sold in June.

Getting Started

Subtract. Regroup if needed.

1. 342
   − 20
   ‾‾‾‾‾

2. 563
   − 50
   ‾‾‾‾‾

3. 245
   − 40
   ‾‾‾‾‾

4. 326
   − 60
   ‾‾‾‾‾

5. 681
   − 90
   ‾‾‾‾‾

Lesson 11-4 • Subtracting Multiples of 10

two hundred five **205**

Practice

Subtract. Regroup if needed.

1. 636 − 80
2. 521 − 20
3. 561 − 80
4. 327 − 50
5. 613 − 20

6. 399 − 30
7. 229 − 50
8. 168 − 70
9. 852 − 90
10. 355 − 50

11. 512 − 70
12. 303 − 50
13. 756 − 30
14. 230 − 30
15. 646 − 60

16. 116 − 20
17. 663 − 80
18. 550 − 70
19. 909 − 40
20. 855 − 60

21. 532 − 50
22. 763 − 40
23. 877 − 90
24. 145 − 30
25. 315 − 70

Problem Solving

Solve.

26. During July there were 325 cars and 70 vans sold. How many more cars than vans were sold?

    _____ more cars

27. There were 257 used cars on the lot. Andrew sold 80. How many cars were left?

    _____ cars

Name _____

Lesson 11-5

Subtracting a 2-Digit From a 3-Digit Number

Tyler School played Bell School in a soccer game. There were 225 students from Tyler and 93 students from Bell attending the game. How many more students from Tyler School attended the game?

We want to know how many more students were from Tyler.

Tyler School had _____ students at the game.

Bell School had _____ students at the game.

To find how many more children were from Tyler, we subtract _____ from _____.

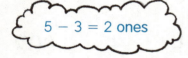

Subtract the ones. Regroup if needed.	Subtract the tens. Regroup if needed.	Subtract the hundreds.
5 − 3 = 2 ones	12 − 9 = 3 tens	1 − 0 = 1 hundred
225 − 93 ――― 2	1 12 2̸2̸5 − 93 ――― 32	1 12 2̸2̸5 − 93 ――― 132

There were _____ more students from Tyler School.

Getting Started

Subtract. Regroup if needed.

1. 346 − 23
2. 346 − 38
3. 346 − 84
4. 579 − 95
5. 718 − 78

Lesson 11-5 • Subtracting a 2-Digit From a 3-Digit Number   two hundred seven **207**

Practice

Subtract. Regroup if needed.

1. 286 − 54
2. 192 − 78
3. 375 − 43
4. 422 − 81
5. 623 − 42

6. 518 − 27
7. 742 − 92
8. 891 − 85
9. 566 − 75
10. 327 − 95

11. 963 − 39
12. 462 − 62
13. 319 − 58
14. 294 − 85
15. 601 − 71

16. 708 − 46
17. 643 − 28
18. 840 − 37
19. 677 − 70
20. 575 − 49

21. 350 − 25
22. 517 − 86
23. 999 − 95
24. 741 − 29
25. 802 − 82

Problem Solving

Solve.

26. Mark jumped rope 395 times. Angie jumped rope only 89 times. How many more times did Mark jump rope?

    _____ times

27. Liz sold 329 tickets to the ballgame. Harry sold 95 tickets. How many more tickets did Liz sell?

    _____ tickets

Name _____

Lesson 11-6

Subtracting 3-Digit Numbers

The Green River Adventures store rents rafts, kayaks, and canoes. How many more rafts than canoes were rented during August?

We want to know how many more rafts than canoes were rented.

There were _____ rafts rented.

There were _____ canoes rented.

To find how many more rafts were rented, we subtract _____ from _____.

Subtract the ones. Regroup if needed.	Subtract the tens. Regroup if needed.	Subtract the hundreds.
10 − 5 = 5 ones	11 − 2 = 9 tens	3 − 2 = 1 hundred
420 − 225 ─── 5	420 − 225 ─── 95	420 − 225 ─── 195

There were _____ more rafts rented.

Getting Started

Subtract. Regroup if needed.

1. 465
   − 243
   ─────

2. 389
   − 164
   ─────

3. 572
   − 155
   ─────

4. 249
   − 164
   ─────

5. 628
   − 139
   ─────

Lesson 11-6 • Subtracting 3-Digit Numbers

Practice

Subtract. Regroup if needed.

1. 965 − 234	2. 782 − 357	3. 359 − 165	4. 417 − 186	5. 531 − 167
6. 361 − 172	7. 619 − 285	8. 999 − 578	9. 843 − 357	10. 775 − 298
11. 375 − 185	12. 658 − 459	13. 583 − 196	14. 417 − 208	15. 625 − 357

Now Try This!

Complete.

1. 100 = __10__ tens

   104 = __10__ tens __4__ ones

   307 = _____ tens _____ ones

   208 = _____ tens _____ ones

   701 = _____ tens _____ one

Trade 1 ten for 10 ones.

2.

tens	ones
~~70~~ 69	~~0~~ 11

tens	ones
50	8

tens	ones
30	2

tens	ones
80	0

Subtract.

3.

tens	ones
80	6
− 34	7

4.

tens	ones
50	7
− 15	8

5.

tens	ones
60	0
− 25	5

6.

tens	ones
80	5
− 59	8

Name _____

Lesson 11-7

Practice Subtracting With 1 or 2 Regroupings

In the holiday parade, there were 452 people marching in bands and 298 in drill teams. How many more people were marching in bands?

We want to know how many more people were in bands.

There were _____ people in bands, and _____ people in drill teams.

To find how many more people were marching in bands, we subtract _____ from _____.

Subtract the ones. Regroup if needed.	Subtract the tens. Regroup if needed.	Subtract the hundreds.
12 − 8 = 4 ones	14 − 9 = 5 tens	3 − 2 = 1 hundred

```
    4 12              14                14
    4̷ 12           3 4̷ 12            3 4̷ 12
   4 5̷ 2           4̷ 5̷ 2̷            4̷ 5̷ 2̷
 −  2 9 8         −  2 9 8          −  2 9 8
   ───────         ───────           ───────
         4              5 4            1 5 4
```

There were _____ more people marching in bands.

Getting Started

Subtract. Regroup if needed.

1. 342 − 29	2. 561 − 71	3. 492 − 175	4. 382 − 7	5. 825 − 598

Lesson 11-7 • Practice Subtracting With 1 or 2 Regroupings

Practice

Subtract. Regroup if needed.

1. 342 − 8
2. 561 − 80
3. 478 − 96
4. 658 − 167
5. 725 − 286

6. 786 − 451
7. 892 − 355
8. 669 − 278
9. 315 − 192
10. 669 − 580

11. 419 − 269
12. 915 − 400
13. 643 − 258
14. 695 − 555
15. 947 − 589

16. 456 − 8
17. 316 − 93
18. 695 − 636
19. 721 − 345
20. 926 − 387

21. 350 − 75
22. 736 − 258
23. 840 − 375
24. 624 − 398
25. 261 − 243

Now Try This!

Put in the missing digits.   *It's Algebra!*

1. 3 5 ☐ − 1 ☐ 2 = 2 3 2
2. 4 ☐ 6 − ☐ 4 ☐ = 2 3 5
3. 7 ☐ 7 − 3 8 ☐ = ☐ 7 3

Name _____

Lesson 11-8

Subtracting Money

Teresa saved $5.46.
She bought a paint set.
How much money does she have left?

We want to find out how much money Teresa has left.

She had _____.

She spent _____.

To find the amount of money she has left, we subtract _____ from _____.

Subtract the pennies. Regroup if needed.	Subtract the dimes. Regroup if needed.	Subtract the dollars.	Put in the dollar sign and decimal point.
3 16 $5.4̸6̸ − 2.57 ——— 9	13 4 3̸ 16 $5̸.4̸6̸ − 2.57 ——— 89	13 4 3̸ 16 $5̸.4̸6̸ − 2.57 ——— 2 89	13 4 3̸ 16 $5̸.4̸6̸ − 2.57 ——— $2.89

Teresa has _____ left.

Getting Started

Subtract. Regroup if needed.

1. $2.94
   − 1.23

2. $5.82
   − 2.65

3. $4.65
   − 1.83

4. $3.14
   − 1.92

5. $5.31
   − 3.45

Lesson 11-8 • Subtracting Money   two hundred thirteen **213**

Practice

Subtract. Regroup if needed.

1. $1.07 − 0.75
2. $4.71 − 1.89
3. $6.35 − 2.75
4. $1.98 − 0.98
5. $7.45 − 1.49

Problem Solving

PAT'S DINER

Hamburger............$2.95	Salad Plate.......$3.49
Ham Sandwich.........$3.25	Milk..............$0.65
Egg Salad Sandwich....$1.88	Chocolate Milk....$0.75
Tuna Sandwich.........$2.59	Iced Tea..........$0.49

Use the menu above.

6. How much more did Jack pay for a hamburger than an egg salad sandwich?

7. How much more is chocolate milk than iced tea?

8. How much did Joe pay for a hamburger and a glass of milk?

9. How much less is a tuna sandwich than a ham sandwich?

10. How much more is a ham sandwich than an egg salad sandwich?

11. How much is a salad plate and a chocolate milk?

Estimating Differences

Maria has $3.02. She buys a ball for $1.08. About how much money does Maria have left?

Round to the nearest ten cents to find out.

Round to the nearest 10 cents.

$3.02 → $3.00
− 1.08 → − 1.10

Estimate.

$3.00
− 1.10
$1.90

Maria has about _____ left.

Getting Started

Estimate. Show how you rounded.

1. Sally has $2.00. She buys a sandwich for $1.38. About how much money does Sally have left? Round to the nearest ten cents.

   _____

2. Mr. Washington has $5.65. He buys a fruit juice for $1.79. About how much money does Mr. Washington have left? Round to the nearest dollar.

   _____

3. Michele has $7.85. She buys a movie ticket for $2.75. About how much money does Michelle have left? Round to the nearest dollar.

   _____

4. Billy spent $3.15 at lunch today. He had $6.92 before lunch. About how much money does Billy have left? Round to the nearest dollar.

   _____

Practice

Estimate. Round to the nearest ten cents.

1. $5.49 − 2.04
2. $6.31 − 3.02
3. $7.84 − 2.17

4. $4.57 − 1.92
5. $9.57 − 4.82
6. $3.35 − 2.11

Estimate. Round to the nearest dollar.

7. $7.22 − 2.38
8. $9.39 − 3.77
9. $7.41 − 2.99

10. $4.21 − 1.83
11. $8.45 − 3.52
12. $6.51 − 3.89

Problem Solving

Estimate. Show how you rounded.

13. The CD that Millie wants to buy is on sale for $7.97. Millie has $9.25. About how much money will Millie have left? Round to the nearest ten cents.

14. Alex was given $7.15 to spend at the mall. He came home with $1.89. About how much did Alex spend? Round to the nearest dollar.

Name _____

Problem Solving Lesson 11-10

It's Algebra!

Problem Solving: Use Logical Reasoning

Here is a riddle:
When you subtract 18 from me, you get 35.
Who am I?

What do you know?

What is the difference? __35__

What is the number being subtracted? _____

You can write an addition problem to find the mystery number.	You can check your answer by using subtraction.
$\begin{array}{r} 35 \\ +18 \\ \hline \end{array}$	$\begin{array}{r} 53 \\ -35 \\ \hline 18 \end{array}$

I am _____.

Getting Started

Solve each riddle.

1. When you subtract me from 28, you get the same number as me.

   Who am I? _____

2. When you subtract 32 from me, you get 45.

   Who am I? _____

3. When you subtract me from 42, you get a number with 1 in the tens place and 2 in the ones place.

   Who am I? _____

4. When 25 is subtracted from me, you get 25.

   Who am I? _____

Lesson 11-10 • Problem Solving: Use Logical Reasoning   two hundred seventeen **217**

Practice

Solve each riddle.

1. If you subtract 35 from me, you get 47.

    Who am I? _____

2. The difference between 60 and me is 20. I am less than 60.

    Who am I? _____

3. If you subtract 22 from me, you get 22.

    Who am I? _____

4. If you subtract 15 from me and then subtract 12 more, you get 43.

    Who am I? _____

5. If you subtract me from 36, you get the same number as me.

    Who am I? _____

6. If you subtract 32 from me and then subtract 23 more, you get 41.

    Who am I? _____

7. If you subtract me from 35, you get 25.

    Who am I? _____

8. If you subtract 17 from me, you get 44.

    Who am I? _____

Now Try This!

Complete each Magic Square.

1.

8		6
	5	
4	9	2

2.

2	9	
7		3
	1	8

3.

2		6
	5	
4		8

Name _____

Chapter 11 Test

Subtract. Regroup if needed.

1. 348 − 9
2. 273 − 6
3. 781 − 50
4. 528 − 70
5. 417 − 60

6. 465 − 81
7. 278 − 90
8. 847 − 35
9. 750 − 23
10. 641 − 78

11. 687 − 55
12. 566 − 59
13. 318 − 135
14. 628 − 435
15. 919 − 378

16. 475 − 149
17. 721 − 254
18. 833 − 126
19. 715 − 359
20. 454 − 168

21. $3.18 − 0.15
22. $2.75 − 1.50
23. $5.75 − 1.56
24. $7.15 − 4.91
25. $6.35 − 2.98

Solve.

26. The pet store had 251 goldfish. Alison sold 163 of them. How many goldfish are left?

    _____ goldfish

27. Kiel had $7.35. He bought a toy boat for $2.45. How much money does he have left?

    _____

Chapter 11 • Test

two hundred nineteen

Cumulative Assessment

Circle the letter of the correct answer.

1 7 + 8	a. 16 b. 14 c. 15 d. NG
2 13 − 6 =	a. 7 b. 3 c. 19 d. NG
3 	a. 55 b. 145 c. 154 d. NG
4 	a. 2:18 b. 2:08 c. 3:18 d. NG
5	a. 42¢ b. 57¢ c. 47¢ d. NG
6 	a. $1.51 b. $1.76 c. $1.71 d. NG

7 57 + 38	a. 21 b. 95 c. 85 d. NG
8 35 + 68	a. 915 b. 33 c. 103 d. NG
9 275 + 465	a. 630 b. 740 c. 730 d. NG
10 71 − 24	a. 47 b. 53 c. 57 d. NG
11 93 − 27	a. 74 b. 76 c. 66 d. NG
12 435 − 162	a. 333 b. 273 c. 373 d. NG

score

Name _____

Chapter 12

Adding and Subtracting 3-Digit Numbers

Lesson 12-1

Adding 3-Digit Numbers

Marilyn and Thomas helped collect paper for the senior citizens' paper drive. How much paper did they collect?

We want to find out how much paper was collected.

Marilyn collected _____ pounds of paper.

Thomas collected _____ pounds of paper.

To find how much paper they collected, we add _____ and _____.

Add the ones. Regroup if needed.	Add the tens. Regroup if needed.	Add the hundreds.
1 237 +285 ――― 2	1 1 237 +285 ――― 22	1 1 237 +285 ――― 522

Marilyn and Thomas collected _____ pounds of paper.

Getting Started

Add.

1. 347
    +212

2. 375
    +374

3. 561
    +327

4. 77
    +18

5. 752
    + 95

6. 96
    +323

7. 606
    +239

8. 154
    +515

9. 809
    + 88

10. 343
    +457

Lesson 12-1 • Adding 3-Digit Numbers

Practice
Add.

1. 618 + 135
2. 515 + 87
3. 156 + 372
4. 612 + 279
5. 350 + 350

6. 175 + 175
7. 149 + 289
8. 649 + 329
9. 233 + 565
10. 578 + 9

11. 219 + 356
12. 317 + 483
13. 86 + 75
14. 529 + 91
15. 490 + 390

16. 96 + 78
17. 775 + 189
18. 89 + 367
19. 455 + 224
20. 496 + 287

21. 634 + 275
22. 398 + 198
23. 758 + 163
24. 239 + 467
25. 683 + 192

Problem Solving
Solve.

26. Clark School has 345 students. Polk School has 488 students. What is the total number of students at both schools?

    _____ students

27. Bonnie collected 159 stickers. Her sister collected 258 stickers. How many stickers did they collect together?

    _____ stickers

222 two hundred twenty-two

Lesson 12-1 • Adding 3-Digit Numbers

Lesson 12-2

Column Addition

It's Algebra!

How many baseball cards did Bobby, Cathleen, and Keith collect altogether?

We want to know how many cards were collected.

Bobby collected _____ cards.

Cathleen collected _____ cards.

Keith collected _____ cards.

To find how many cards in all, we add _____, _____, and _____.

Baseball Cards Collected:
Bobby......126
Cathleen...252
Keith......375

Add the ones. Regroup if needed.	Add the tens. Regroup if needed.	Add the hundreds.
$\begin{array}{r} \overset{1}{1}26 \\ 252 \\ +375 \\ \hline 3 \end{array}$	$\begin{array}{r} \overset{1\,1}{1}26 \\ 252 \\ +375 \\ \hline 53 \end{array}$	$\begin{array}{r} \overset{1\,1}{1}26 \\ 252 \\ +375 \\ \hline 753 \end{array}$

They collected _____ baseball cards altogether.

Getting Started

Add.

1. 113
   231
   +442

2. 143
    46
   + 51

3. 314
   122
   +351

4. 442
   136
   + 55

5. 165
   225
   +365

6. 251
   315
   +178

7. 423
    74
   +186

8. 142
   436
   +219

9. 323
   265
   +188

10. 504
    193
    +268

Lesson 12-2 • Column Addition   two hundred twenty-three **223**

Practice

Add.

1.	511 330 +145	2.	232 27 + 47	3.	314 85 +200	4.	125 54 +397	5.	325 132 +538
6.	534 134 +237	7.	415 162 +244	8.	241 367 +179	9.	321 465 +212	10.	165 316 +273
11.	923 56 + 19	12.	86 202 +658	13.	192 505 +247	14.	434 143 +309	15.	107 581 +270

Now Try This!

Fill in the missing numbers.   *It's Algebra!*

1. 3 4 6
    + ☐ ☐ ☐
    ─────
      7 9 8

2.   2 ☐ 5
    + ☐ 6 ☐
    ─────
      8 8 8

3. ☐ 9 3
    + 4 ☐ 1
    ─────
      9 7 4

4. 3 2 7
    + ☐ 5 ☐
    ─────
      8 8 3

5. ☐ 9 ☐
    + 3 4 2
    ─────
      7 3 9

6. ☐ 3 ☐
    + 1 ☐ 9
    ─────
      9 9 0

Name _____

Lesson 12-3

Subtracting 3-Digit Numbers

How much farther is it from Kent to Benson than from Benson to Jackson?

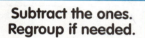

We want to find out how much farther it is from Kent to Benson.

It is _____ miles from Kent to Benson.

It is _____ miles from Benson to Jackson.

To find how much farther, we subtract _____ from _____.

Subtract the ones. Regroup if needed.	Subtract the tens. Regroup if needed.	Subtract the hundreds.
2 15 6̸3̸5̸ − 4 5 7 ───── 　　8	12 5 2̸ 15 6̸3̸5̸ − 4 5 7 ───── 　7 8	12 5 2̸ 15 6̸3̸5̸ − 4 5 7 ───── 1 7 8

It is _____ miles farther from Kent to Benson.

Getting Started

Subtract. Regroup if needed.

1. 347   2. 845   3. 561   4. 877   5. 752
   − 212   − 428   − 327   − 18   − 95

6. 275   7. 323   8. 515   9. 457   10. 635
   − 198   − 96   − 154   − 289   − 436

Lesson 12-3 • Subtracting 3-Digit Numbers   two hundred twenty-five **225**

Practice

Subtract. Regroup if needed.

1. 648 − 234
2. 435 − 365
3. 741 − 329
4. 318 − 175
5. 526 − 143

6. 227 − 88
7. 398 − 200
8. 921 − 567
9. 847 − 436
10. 733 − 227

11. 490 − 170
12. 529 − 91
13. 654 − 234
14. 465 − 165
15. 624 − 375

16. 647 − 432
17. 518 − 279
18. 422 − 87
19. 882 − 693
20. 753 − 275

Problem Solving

Solve.

21. Some fishing boats brought in 256 fish on Thursday and 428 fish on Friday. How many more fish were caught on Friday?

    _____ fish

22. Gene's father stacked 375 logs. Gene stacked 187 logs. How many more logs did his father stack?

    _____ logs

Name _____

Lesson 12-4

Practice Subtracting 3-Digit Numbers

During the spring sale, the Sports Store sold 325 baseballs and 179 footballs. How many more baseballs were sold?

We want to know how many more baseballs were sold.

There were ____ baseballs sold.

There were ____ footballs sold.

To find how many more baseballs were sold, we subtract ____ from ____.

Subtract the ones. Regroup if needed.	Subtract the tens. Regroup if needed.	Subtract the hundreds.
$\begin{array}{r} 115 \\ 3\cancel{2}\cancel{5} \\ -179 \\ \hline 6 \end{array}$	$\begin{array}{r} 11 \\ 2\cancel{1}15 \\ \cancel{3}\cancel{2}\cancel{5} \\ -179 \\ \hline 46 \end{array}$	$\begin{array}{r} 11 \\ 2\cancel{1}15 \\ \cancel{3}\cancel{2}\cancel{5} \\ -179 \\ \hline 146 \end{array}$

The store sold ____ more baseballs than footballs.

Getting Started

Subtract. Regroup if needed.

1. 465 − 128
2. 819 − 96
3. 752 − 329
4. 530 − 156
5. 738 − 299

6. 561 − 9
7. 678 − 496
8. 788 − 298
9. 937 − 447
10. 825 − 466

Practice

Subtract. Regroup if needed.

1. 578 − 294
2. 428 − 183
3. 687 − 269
4. 824 − 470
5. 633 − 156

6. 258 − 85
7. 755 − 255
8. 515 − 347
9. 786 − 395
10. 678 − 493

11. 714 − 529
12. 337 − 165
13. 758 − 132
14. 621 − 279
15. 582 − 298

Now Try This!

Solve each problem.

Start with 225.

Add 126.   + 126

351

Subtract 38.

Add 87.

Start with 396.

Add 275.

Subtract 385.

Add 214.

Checking Subtraction

You can check subtraction by adding.

Subtract.	Add to check.

```
    1 1
  6 15
  7̷2̷5̷         458
 -267        +267
  458         725
```

Getting Started

Subtract. Check your answers.

1. 83   48
   −35   +35
   ‾‾‾   ‾‾‾
    48   83

2. 145
   − 18
   ‾‾‾‾

3. 367
   −139
   ‾‾‾‾

Copy and subtract. Then check your answers.

4. 348 − 127 = ___

5. 475 − 298 = ___

Practice

Subtract. Check your answers.

1. 522 − 271
2. 78 − 43
3. 157 − 29
4. 645 − 298
5. 849 − 587
6. 731 − 285

Copy and subtract. Then check your answers.

7. 627 − 345 = ___
8. 517 − 209 = ___
9. 839 − 468 = ___
10. 755 − 388 = ___

Now Try This!

Use these digits to complete each subtraction problem. 4 8 6

1. 6 8 − ☐ = 6 4
2. ☐ ☐ − 6 = 7 8
3. ☐ ☐ − ☐ = 3 8
4. ☐ ☐ − ☐ = 5 6

Name _____

Lesson 12-6

Subtracting Money

How much more does the car cost than the boat?

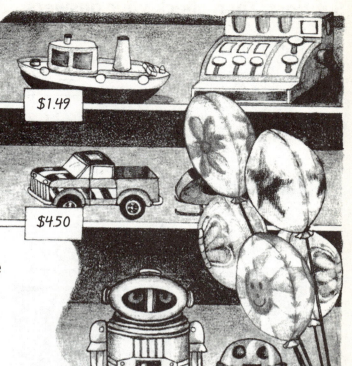

We want to know how much more the car costs.

The cost of the car is _____.

The cost of the boat is _____.

To find how much more the car costs, we subtract _____ from _____.

Copy the problem. Line up the points.	Subtract. Regroup if needed.	Put in the dollar sign and decimal point.	Add to check.
$3.25 − 1.49	$³̷2̷.¹⁵2̷5̷ − 1.49 1 76	$³̷2̷.¹⁵2̷5̷ − 1.49 $1.76	¹ ¹ $1.76 + 1.49 $3.25

The car costs _____ more than the boat.

Getting Started

Subtract. Then check your answers.

1. $4.27
  − 1.15

2. $5.32
  − 2.29

3. $6.25
  − 4.75

Lesson 12-6 • Subtracting Money   two hundred thirty-one **231**

Practice

Subtract. Then check your answers.

1. $7.46 − 3.98

2. $9.29 − 6.37

3. $8.54 − 5.75

Problem Solving

 $3.85 STARS
 $5.29 CHECKERS
 $7.50
 $1.98

Solve.

4. How much would you pay for a book and a game?

5. How much more would you pay for a robot than a boat?

6. How much more does a game cost than a book?

7. If you bought a game and you gave the clerk $5.50, how much change would you get?

8. How much would you pay for a robot and a boat?

9. How much more would you pay for a book than a boat?

Name _____

Problem Solving
Lesson 12-7

Problem Solving: Use Data From a Picture

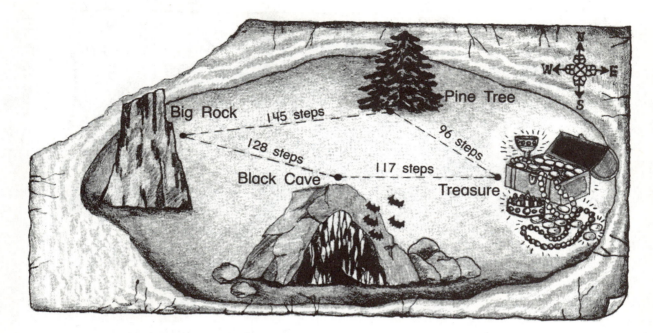

Solve.

1. How many steps would you walk from Big Rock to Pine Tree to the Treasure?

   _____ steps

2. How many steps is it from Big Rock to Black Cave to the Treasure?

   _____ steps

3. How much farther is it from Big Rock to Pine Tree than from Pine Tree to the Treasure?

   _____ steps

4. How much farther is it from Big Rock to Black Cave than from Black Cave to the Treasure?

   _____ steps

5. How much farther is it from Big Rock to Pine Tree than from Big Rock to Black Cave?

   _____ steps

6. How much farther is it from Black Cave to the Treasure than from Pine Tree to the Treasure?

   _____ steps

Lesson 12-7 • Problem Solving: Use Data From a Picture   two hundred thirty-three **233**

Apply

Solve.

1. How many steps would you walk from the school to the store to the post office?

   _____ steps

2. How many steps would you walk from the post office to the park and back to the post office?

   _____ steps

3. How many steps would you walk from the park to the school to the store?

   _____ steps

4. How much farther is it from the school to the store than from the store to the post office?

   _____ steps

5. How much farther is it from the school to the park than from the post office to the park?

   _____ steps

6. How much farther is it from the store to the post office than from the park to the post office?

   _____ steps

Name _____

Chapter 12 Test

Add or subtract.

1. 276
  + 23

2. 357
  + 28

3. 515
  − 48

4. 148
  + 347

5. 259
  + 620

6. 468
    132
  + 375

7. 206
    280
  + 214

8. 383
    115
  + 129

9. 685
  + 133

10. 767
  − 258

11. 873
  − 395

12. 931
  − 567

13. 472
  − 274

14. $3.95
  + 1.22

15. $5.25
  + 3.29

16. $8.34
  − 2.49

17. $6.15
  − 2.37

Subtract. Then check your answers.

18. $5.69
  − 2.87

19. 346
  − 157

20. $7.53
  − 2.75

Solve.

21. Ling had $5.75. He spent $1.89. How much money does he have left?

    Ling has _____ left.

22. Jane had $3.75. She earned $2.95. How much money does she have now?

    Jane has _____.

Chapter 12 • Test   two hundred thirty-five **235**

Cumulative Assessment

Circle the letter of the correct answer.

① 7 + 8 =
 a. 1
 b. 15
 c. 14
 d. NG

② 16
− 7
 a. 9
 b. 23
 c. 19
 d. NG

③
 a. 326
 b. 263
 c. 236
 d. NG

④
 a. $1.88
 b. $1.28
 c. $1.83
 d. NG

⑤
 a. 4:45
 b. 3:45
 c. 9:18
 d. NG

⑥ 85
+ 67
 a. 12
 b. 142
 c. 152
 d. NG

⑦ 238
+ 475
 a. 703
 b. 603
 c. 713
 d. NG

⑧ 91
− 48
 a. 53
 b. 43
 c. 57
 d. NG

⑨ 315
− 197
 a. 118
 b. 512
 c. 328
 d. NG

⑩ 563
− 274
 a. 281
 b. 311
 c. 399
 d. NG

⑪ $3.25
+ 2.75
 a. $6.00
 b. $5.90
 c. $5.00
 d. NG

⑫ $5.25
− 2.98
 a. $8.23
 b. $2.27
 c. $3.37
 d. NG

score

236 two hundred thirty-six

Chapter 12 • Cumulative Assessment

Geometry and Fractions

Chapter 13
Lesson 13-1

Solid Figures

Match each shape to its name.

1.
2.

sphere

3.
4.

cube

5.
6.

cylinder

7.
8.

cone

Lesson 13-1 • Solid Figures

two hundred thirty-seven 237

Practice

Circle the shapes that match the first shape in each row.

1.  cone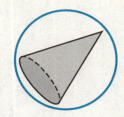

2. cube

3.  cylinder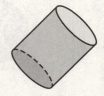

4. sphere

5.  pyramid

6.  cone

Lesson 13-1 • Solid Figures

Lesson 13-2

Faces, Vertices, and Edges

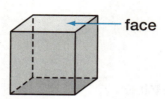

A cube has 6 faces.

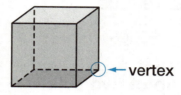

A cube has 8 vertices, or corners.

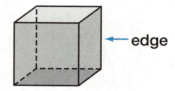

A cube has 12 edges.

Getting Started

How many faces, vertices, and edges does each shape have?

1.
pyramid
___ faces
___ vertices
___ edges

2.
rectangular prism
___ faces
___ vertices
___ edges

3.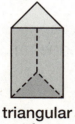
triangular prism
___ faces
___ vertices
___ edges

4.
sphere
___ faces
___ vertices
___ edges

Lesson 13-2 • Faces, Vertices, and Edges   two hundred thirty-nine **239**

Practice

Count the number of faces, vertices, and edges in each shape.

1.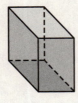
   ___ faces
   ___ vertices
   ___ edges

2.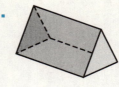
   ___ faces
   ___ vertices
   ___ edges

Each object is made up of two solid shapes. Name each shape.

3.
   _____
   _____

4.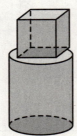
   _____
   _____

5.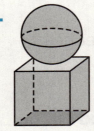
   _____
   _____

Now Try This!

Answer each riddle. Then draw the shape.

1. I have 5 faces, 6 vertices, and 9 edges. What shape am I?

   _____

2. I have no faces, vertices, and edges. What shape am I?

   _____

3. I have 6 faces, 8 vertices, and 12 edges. What shape am I?

   _____

4. I have 5 faces, 5 vertices, and 8 edges. What shape am I?

   _____

Name _____

Lesson 13-3

Plane Figures

 circle

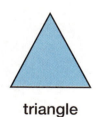 triangle

 square

 rectangle

Put C inside each circle.   **Put S inside each square.**

Put T inside each triangle.   **Put R inside each rectangle.**

Lesson 13-3 • Plane Figures   two hundred forty-one **241**

Practice

Color the circles green.   Color the triangles purple.

Color the squares red.   Color the rectangles orange.

Lesson 13-3 • Plane Figures

Slides, Flips, and Turns

You can move figures in different ways.

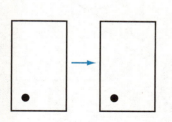
This is a slide.

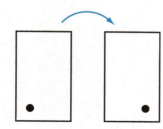
This is a flip.

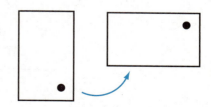
This is a turn.

Getting Started

Describe how each figure moved.

1.
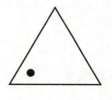
   turn

2.
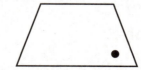
   _____

3.
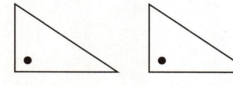
   _____

4.
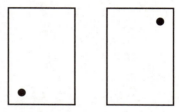
   _____

Lesson 13-4 • Slides, Flips, and Turns   two hundred forty-three **243**

Practice

Describe how each figure moved.

1.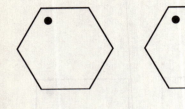
   _____

2.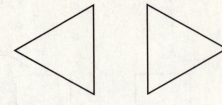
   _____

3.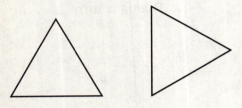
   _____

4.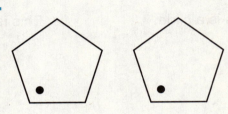
   _____

Now Try This!

Draw a picture to solve.

1. How does the letter E look when you flip it? Draw it.

2. What letter can you make by turning an M? Draw it.

244 two hundred forty-four · Lesson 13-4 • Slides, Flips, and Turns

Name _____

Lesson 13-5

Symmetry

If you fold along a line of symmetry, the two parts will match exactly.

A line of symmetry

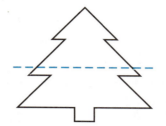
Not a line of symmetry

Is it a line of symmetry? Circle yes or no.

1.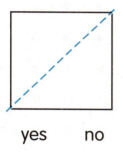
   yes   no

2.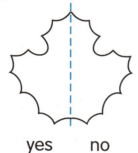
   yes   no

3.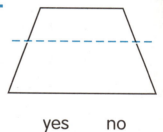
   yes   no

4.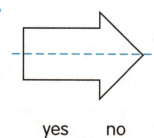
   yes   no

5.
   yes   no

6.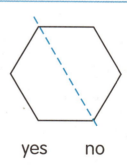
   yes   no

7.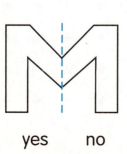
   yes   no

8.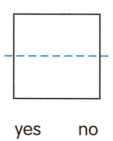
   yes   no

9.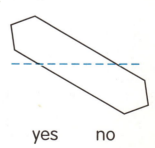
   yes   no

Lesson 13-5 • Symmetry

two hundred forty-five **245**

Practice

The line of symmetry in each figure shows one part of a symmetric figure. Draw the missing part of each figure.

1.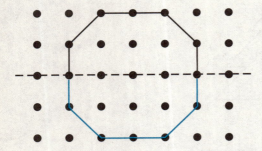

2.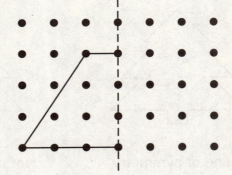

3.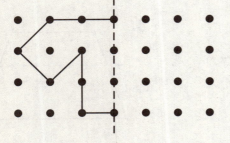

4.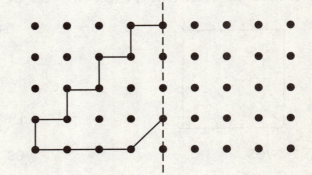

5.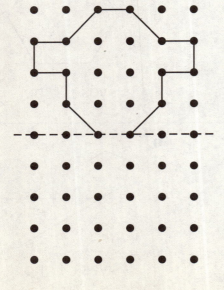

6.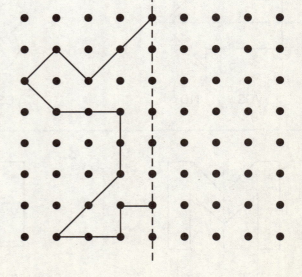

Name _____

Lesson 13-6

Fractions

halves
$\frac{1}{2}$ ← blue part
← equal parts

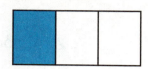
thirds
$\frac{1}{3}$ ← blue part
← equal parts

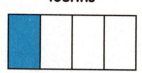
fourths
$\frac{1}{4}$ ← blue part
← equal parts

What part is colored blue? Circle the correct fraction.

1.
$\frac{1}{2}$ $\frac{1}{3}$ $\frac{1}{4}$

2.
$\frac{1}{2}$ $\frac{1}{3}$ $\frac{1}{4}$

3.
$\frac{1}{2}$ $\frac{1}{3}$ $\frac{1}{4}$

4.
$\frac{1}{3}$ $\frac{1}{4}$ $\frac{1}{5}$

5.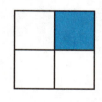
$\frac{1}{2}$ $\frac{1}{3}$ $\frac{1}{4}$

6.
$\frac{1}{2}$ $\frac{1}{3}$ $\frac{1}{4}$

7.
$\frac{1}{2}$ $\frac{1}{3}$ $\frac{1}{4}$

8.
$\frac{1}{2}$ $\frac{1}{3}$ $\frac{1}{4}$

9.
$\frac{1}{3}$ $\frac{1}{4}$ $\frac{1}{5}$

10.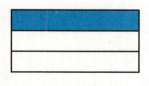
$\frac{1}{2}$ $\frac{1}{3}$ $\frac{1}{4}$

11.
$\frac{1}{2}$ $\frac{1}{3}$ $\frac{1}{4}$

12.
$\frac{1}{2}$ $\frac{1}{3}$ $\frac{1}{4}$

Practice

1. Color $\frac{1}{2}$.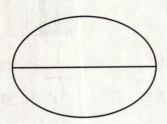

2. Color $\frac{1}{4}$.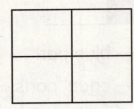

3. Color $\frac{1}{3}$.

4. Color $\frac{1}{2}$.

5. Color $\frac{1}{4}$.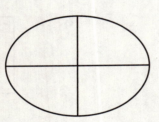

6. Color $\frac{1}{5}$.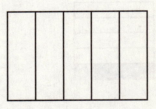

7. Color $\frac{1}{2}$.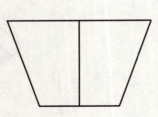

8. Color $\frac{1}{3}$.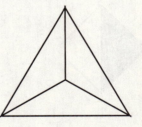

9. Color $\frac{1}{3}$.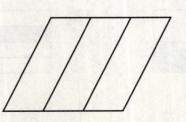

10. Color $\frac{1}{12}$.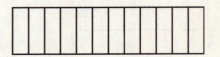

Fractional Parts

Lesson 13-7

3 blue parts

4 equal parts

$\frac{3}{4}$ of the circle is blue.

What part is blue? Write the fraction.

1.

2.

3.

4.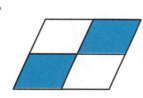

5.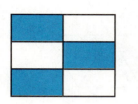

6.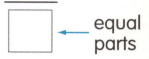

7.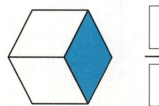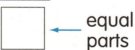

8.

Practice

1. Color $\frac{2}{3}$.
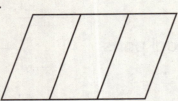

2. Color $\frac{1}{5}$.

3. Color $\frac{3}{4}$.
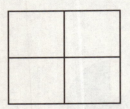

4. Color $\frac{3}{6}$.
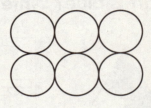

5. Color $\frac{2}{5}$.
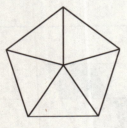

6. Color $\frac{1}{3}$.
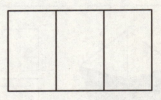

7. Color $\frac{3}{4}$.

8. Color $\frac{5}{6}$.
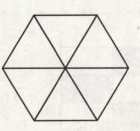

9. Color $\frac{5}{8}$.

10. Color $\frac{4}{5}$.
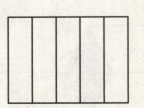

Name _____

Lesson 13-8

Parts of a Whole

$\frac{1}{4}$ is white.

$\frac{3}{4}$ is blue.

Color the parts.

1. Color $\frac{1}{6}$ red.
   Color $\frac{5}{6}$ blue.
   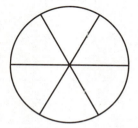

2. Color $\frac{2}{3}$ purple.
   Color $\frac{1}{3}$ yellow.

3. Color $\frac{3}{8}$ blue.
   Color $\frac{5}{8}$ green.
   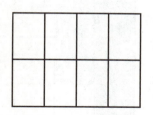

4. Color $\frac{7}{10}$ brown.
   Color $\frac{3}{10}$ yellow.
   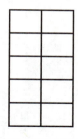

5. Color $\frac{3}{5}$ purple.
   Color $\frac{2}{5}$ yellow.
   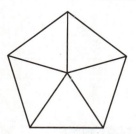

6. Color $\frac{2}{4}$ red.
   Color $\frac{2}{4}$ blue.
   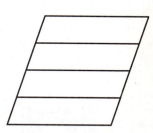

7. Color $\frac{1}{3}$ red.
   Color $\frac{2}{3}$ blue.
   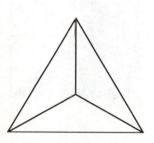

8. Color $\frac{5}{12}$ purple.
   Color $\frac{7}{12}$ yellow.
   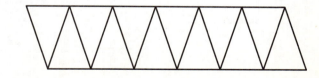

Lesson 13-8 • Parts of a Whole

Practice

Write the fraction that tells which part is blue.
Then write the fraction that tells which part is white.

1.
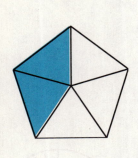

$\dfrac{2}{5}$ is blue.

$\dfrac{3}{5}$ is white.

2.
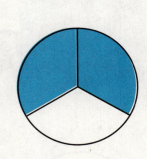

___ is blue.

___ is white.

3.
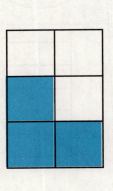

___ is blue.

___ is white.

4.
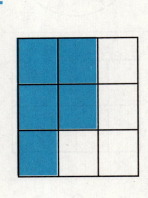

___ is blue.

___ is white.

5.
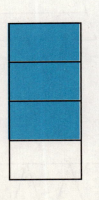

___ is blue.

___ is white.

6.
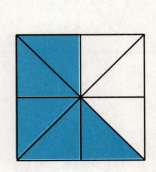

___ is blue.

___ is white.

Lesson 13-8 • Parts of a Whole

Lesson 13-9

Parts of a Group With the Same Objects

Ann has 5 cars. 3 cars are blue. What part of the cars are blue?

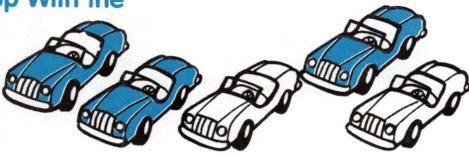

There are ____ blue cars.

There are ____ cars in all.

―
 of the cars are blue.

1. Color $\frac{1}{2}$ of the apples.

2. Color $\frac{2}{3}$ of the oranges.

3. Color $\frac{4}{5}$ of the bananas.

4. Color $\frac{3}{10}$ of the cherries.

5. Color $\frac{3}{4}$ of the tomatoes.

6. Color $\frac{3}{6}$ of the peaches.

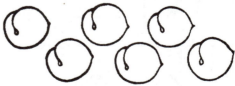

7. Color $\frac{4}{4}$ of the pears.

8. Color $\frac{5}{8}$ of the lemons.

Practice

What part is blue? Write the fraction.

1. 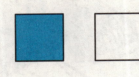 $\frac{1}{2}$

2.  ___

3. 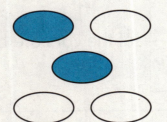 ___

4. 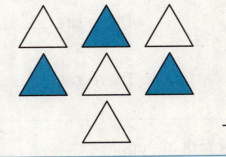 ___

5. 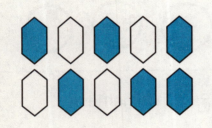 ___

6. 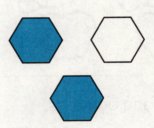 ___

7. 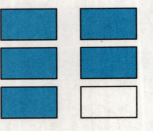 ___

8. 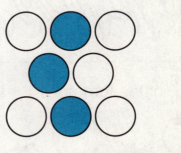 ___

9. 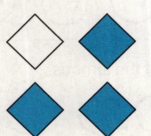 ___

10. 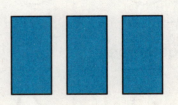 ___

Name _____

Lesson 13-10

Parts of a Group With Different Objects

Alfredo asked 10 of his friends which flavor of ice cream they like. He made a Venn diagram from the information.

We can use the Venn diagram to find what fraction of his friends like vanilla.

How many friends are there in all? __10__

How many friends like only vanilla? __4__

How many friends like both vanilla and chocolate? _____

What fraction of students like vanilla? _____

FAVORITE ICE CREAM FLAVORS

Getting Started

Use the Venn diagram to find each fraction.

1. What fraction of friends like both vanilla and chocolate ice cream?

   _____ friends

2. What fraction of friends like only chocolate ice cream?

   _____ friends

3. What fraction of friends like chocolate ice cream?

   _____ friends

4. What fraction of friends like only vanilla ice cream?

   _____ friends

Lesson 13-10 • Parts of a Group With Different Objects

Practice

Use the Venn diagram to find each fraction.

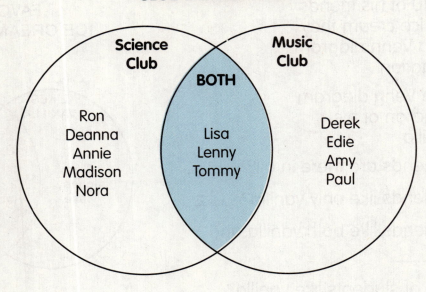

1. What fraction of students are only in the Science Club?

   _____ students

2. What fraction of students are in the Science Club?

   _____ students

3. What fraction of students are only in the Music Club?

   _____ students

4. What fraction of students are in the Music Club?

   _____ students

5. What fraction of students are involved in both clubs?

   _____ students

6. What fraction of students belong to at least 1 club?

   _____ students

Name _____

**Problem Solving
Lesson 13-11**

Problem Solving: Draw a Picture

There are 4 cats. 3 of the cats have stripes. What fraction of the cats have stripes? You can use a picture to show the fraction.

How many cats are there? __4__

How many of the cats have stripes? _____

What fraction of the cats have stripes? _____

Getting Started

Draw a picture to solve.

1. There are 3 coins. 2 of the coins are quarters. What fraction of the coins are quarters?

   _____

2. There are 5 balls. 3 of the balls are footballs. The rest are baseballs. What fraction of the balls are footballs?

   _____

3. There are 4 students on the team. 2 of the students are girls. What fraction of the team are girls?

   _____

Practice

Draw a picture to solve.

1. A pizza has 8 slices. Juan ate $\frac{3}{8}$ of a pizza. What fraction of the pizza did he leave?

    _____

2. There are 5 children on the basketball team. 4 are boys. What fraction of the team are girls?

    _____

3. There are 6 circles. 2 of the circles are shaded. What fraction of the circles are shaded?

    _____

4. Brian has 8 shirts. $\frac{6}{8}$ of his shirts have stripes. What fraction of Brian's shirts do not have stripes?

    _____

5. A rectangle is divided into 4 equal parts. One part is shaded. What fraction of the rectangle is not shaded?

    _____

Name _____

Chapter 13 Test

How many of each shape are there? Write the number.

1. _____ circles
2. _____ triangles
3. _____ squares
4. _____ rectangles

Write the number for each.

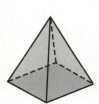

5. _____ faces
6. _____ vertices
7. _____ edges

Is the line a line of symmetry? Circle yes or no.

8.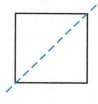

   yes   no

9.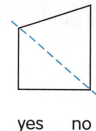

   yes   no

Write the fraction for the blue parts of each figure.

10. 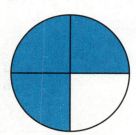 _____

11. 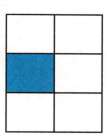 _____

12. 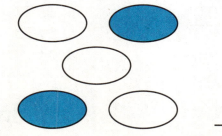 _____

13. 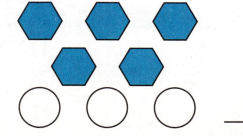 _____

Chapter 13 • Test

two hundred fifty-nine **259**

Cumulative Assessment

Circle the letter of the correct answer.

1. 5 + 7 =
   a. 2
   b. 12
   c. 13
   d. NG

2. 15 − 8
   a. 23
   b. 3
   c. 7
   d. NG

3.
   a. 352
   b. 235
   c. 523
   d. NG

4. 35 + 27 =
   a. 52
   b. 8
   c. 62
   d. NG

5. 473 + 75
   a. 448
   b. 548
   c. 398
   d. NG

6. 265 + 376
   a. 641
   b. 631
   c. 541
   d. NG

7. 85 − 26
   a. 61
   b. 59
   c. 69
   d. NG

8. 526 − 85
   a. 561
   b. 541
   c. 441
   d. NG

9. 725 − 298
   a. 573
   b. 427
   c. 537
   d. NG

10. What part is blue?
    a. $\frac{3}{4}$
    b. $\frac{4}{3}$
    c. $\frac{1}{4}$
    d. NG

11. 455 + 345
    a. 800
    b. 750
    c. 700
    d. NG

12. $4.59 + 2.82
    a. $7.31
    b. $6.41
    c. $7.41
    d. NG

13. $7.15 − 0.48
    a. $6.67
    b. $6.77
    c. $7.33
    d. NG

score

Measurement

Chapter 14

Lesson 14-1

Inches and Feet

You can use an inch ruler to measure how many inches long an object is.

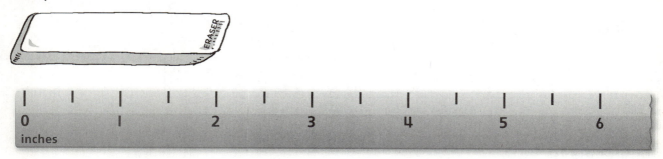

An eraser is 2 inches long.

There are 12 inches in 1 foot. A ruler is 1 foot long.

1 foot = 12 inches

Getting Started

Decide if you would measure each object in inches or feet. Circle your answer.

1.

(inches)   feet

2.

inches   feet

3.

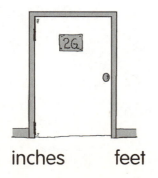

inches   feet

4.

inches   feet

Lesson 14-1 • Inches and Feet

two hundred sixty-one **261**

Practice

Mark each cut.

$3\frac{1}{2}$ inches

1.

2 inches

2.

4 inches

3.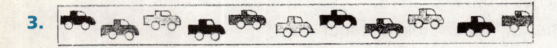

3 inches

4.

Now Try This!

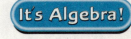

A yard is equal to 3 feet. There are 36 inches in a yard. Use this information to complete the following.

1. 1 yard = __3__ feet
2. 1 yard = ____ inches
3. 2 yards = ____ feet
4. 2 yards = ____ inches
5. Estimate the length of your classroom in yards. ____ yards

Name _____

Lesson 14-2

Measuring to the Nearest Inch

Raul wants to find the length of his pencil to the nearest inch.

He can estimate the length. The pencil is about __5__ inches long.

Getting Started

Use your inch ruler. Estimate each length to the nearest inch.

1.

   It is between ___ and ___ inches.   ___ nearest inch

2.

   It is between ___ and ___ inches.   ___ nearest inch

3.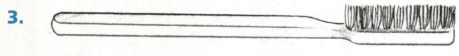

   It is between ___ and ___ inches.   ___ nearest inch

4.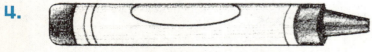

   It is between ___ and ___ inches.   ___ nearest inch

Lesson 14-2 • Measuring to the Nearest Inch   two hundred sixty-three **263**

Practice

Use your inch ruler. Estimate each length to the nearest inch.

1.

    It is between ____ and ____ inches. ____ nearest inch

2.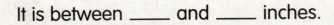

    It is between ____ and ____ inches. ____ nearest inch

3.

    It is between ____ and ____ inches. ____ nearest inch

4.

    It is between ____ and ____ inches. ____ nearest inch

5.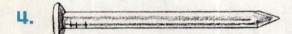

    It is between ____ and ____ inches. ____ nearest inch

6.

    It is between ____ and ____ inches. ____ nearest inch

7.

    It is between ____ and ____ inches. ____ nearest inch

Lesson 14-3

Pounds and Ounces

A pound is a unit of weight.

An ounce is also a unit of weight.

16 ounces = 1 pound

Getting Started

Circle the better estimate.

1.

   (More than 1 pound)

   Less than 1 pound

2.

   More than 1 pound

   Less than 1 pound

3.

   2 pounds   2 ounces

4.

   4 pounds   4 ounces

Lesson 14-3 • Pounds and Ounces

two hundred sixty-five **265**

Practice

Circle the better estimate.

1.

   More than 1 pound

   Less than 1 pound

2.

   More than 1 pound

   Less than 1 pound

3.

   More than 1 pound

   Less than 1 pound

4.

   More than 1 pound

   Less than 1 pound

5.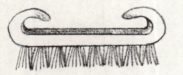

   3 pounds   3 ounces

6.

   20 pounds   20 ounces

7.

   21 pounds   21 ounces

8.

   1 pound   1 ounce

9.

   3 pounds   3 ounces

10.

    15 pounds   15 ounces

Name _____

Lesson 14-4

Cups, Pints, and Quarts

2 cups will fill 1 pint.   2 pints will fill 1 quart.   4 cups will fill 1 quart.

Getting Started

Circle the better estimate.

1. mug of milk

(1 cup)   1 quart

2. bowl of cereal

2 cups   2 pints

3. pitcher of water

1 pint   1 quart

4. fishbowl

4 pints   4 quarts

Circle the correct number of containers.

5.  will fill

6.  will fill

Lesson 14-4 • Cups, Pints, and Quarts

two hundred sixty-seven **267**

Practice

Circle the better estimate.

1. coffee pot

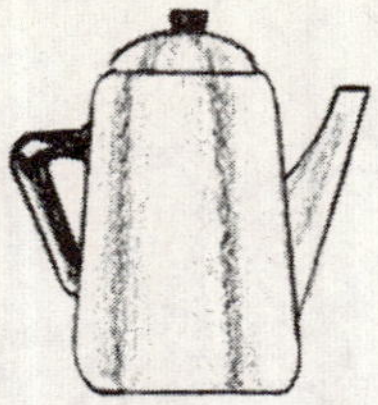

8 cups 8 quarts

2. baking pan

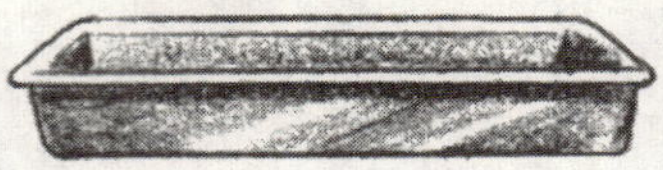

2 cups 2 quarts

3. can of juice

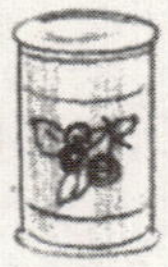

2 cups 2 pints

4. water bucket

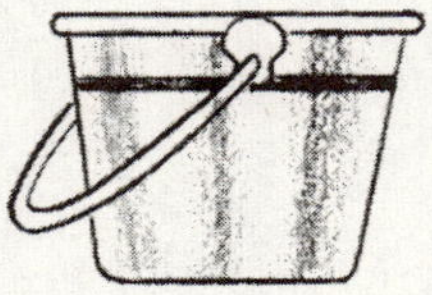

4 quarts 4 cups

Circle the correct number of containers.

5.

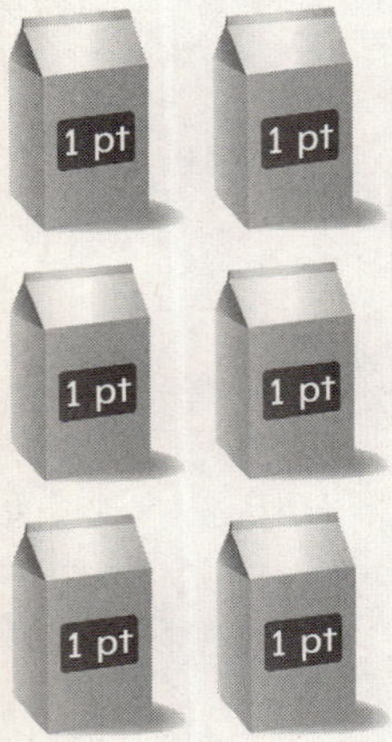

will fill

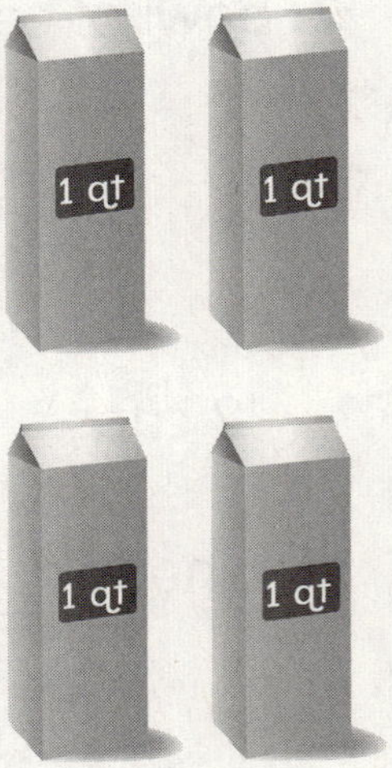

6.

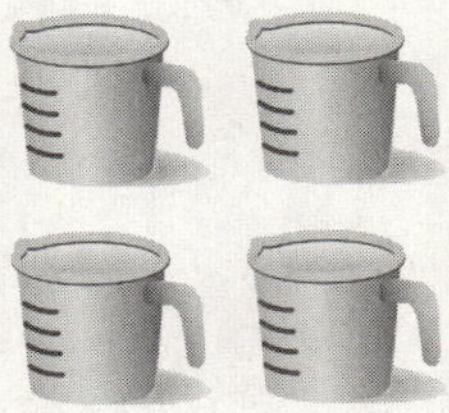

will fill

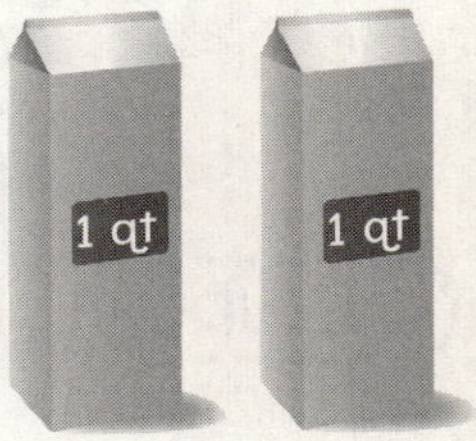

7.

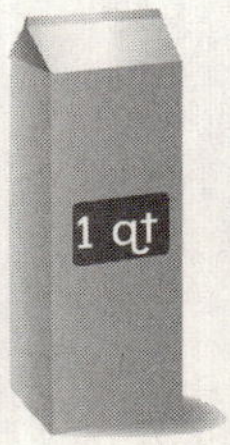

will fill

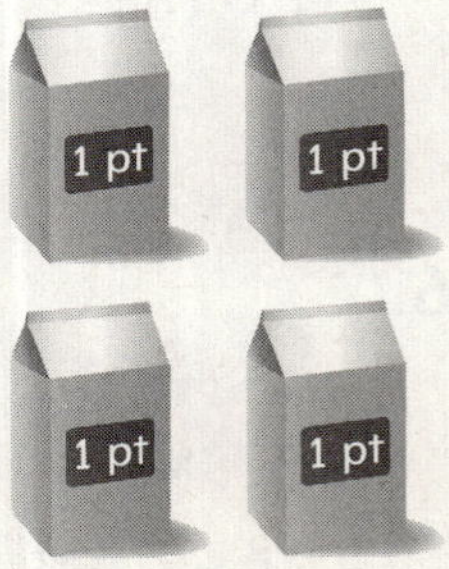

8.

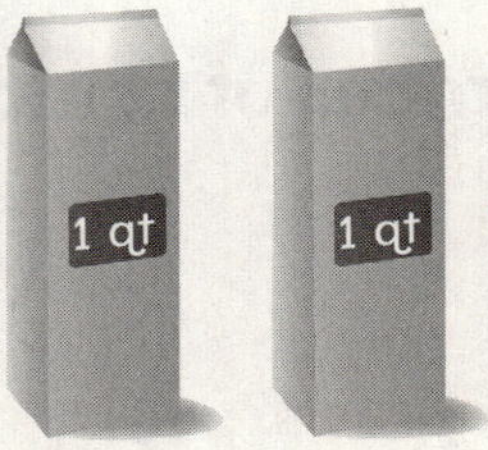

will fill

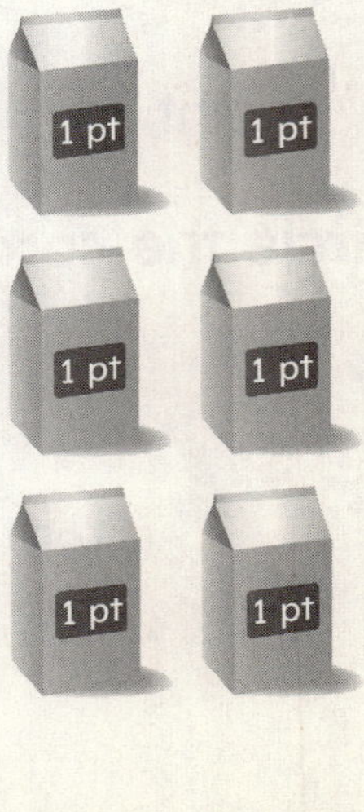

Name _____

Lesson 14-5

Centimeters and Meters

You can use a centimeter ruler to measure how many centimeters long an object is.

A paper clip is $4\frac{1}{2}$ centimeters long.

There are 100 centimeters in 1 meter. You can use a meterstick to measure how many meters an object is.

1 meter = 100 centimeters

Getting Started

Decide if you would use a centimeter ruler or a meterstick to measure each object. Circle your answer.

1.

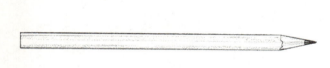

(centimeter ruler)   meterstick

2.

centimeter ruler   meterstick

3.

centimeter ruler   meterstick

4.

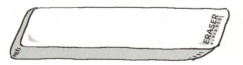

centimeter ruler   meterstick

Practice

Mark each cut.

5 centimeters

1.

9 centimeters

2.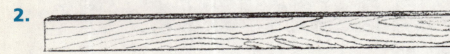

7 centimeters

3.

Use your centimeter ruler. Find the lengths.

4.  ____ centimeters

5. ____ centimeters

6.  ____ centimeters

> **Now Try This!**
>
> **Circle the longer length.**
> **Remember, there are 100 centimeters in 1 meter.**
>
> 1. (235 centimeters)   1 meter
> 2. 10 centimeters   1 meter
> 3. 99 centimeters   2 meters
> 4. 300 centimeters   2 meters

Name _____

Lesson 14-6

Measuring to the Nearest Centimeter

Seth wants to know about how long the nail is. He uses his centimeter ruler to measure to the nearest centimeter.

The length is between 6 and 7 centimeters.

The nail is between ____ and ____ centimeters.

____ nearest centimeter

Getting Started

Use your centimeter ruler. Estimate each length to the nearest centimeter.

1.

It is between ____ and ____ centimeters.

____ nearest centimeter

2.

It is between ____ and ____ centimeters.

____ nearest centimeter

3.

It is between ____ and ____ centimeters.

____ nearest centimeter

4.

It is between ____ and ____ centimeters.

____ nearest centimeter

Lesson 14-6 • Measuring to the Nearest Centimeter

two hundred seventy-one

Practice

Use your centimeter ruler. Estimate each length to the nearest centimeter.

1.

   It is between ____ and ____ centimeters.   ____
   nearest centimeter

2.

   It is between ____ and ____ centimeters.   ____
   nearest centimeter

3.

   It is between ____ and ____ centimeters.   ____
   nearest centimeter

4.

   It is between ____ and ____ centimeters.   ____
   nearest centimeter

5.

   It is between ____ and ____ centimeters.   ____
   nearest centimeter

6.

   It is between ____ and ____ centimeters.   ____
   nearest centimeter

7.

   It is between ____ and ____ centimeters.   ____
   nearest centimeter

Name _____

Lesson 14-7

Grams and Kilograms

A kilogram is a metric unit for measuring how much something weighs.
The book weighs 1 kilogram.

A baseball bat weighs less than 1 kilogram.
A bowling ball weighs more than 1 kilogram.

A gram is also a metric unit for measuring how much something weighs.

There are 1,000 grams in a kilogram.
1,000 grams = 1 kilogram

Getting Started

Circle the better estimate.

1.

(More than 1 kilogram)
Less than 1 kilogram

2.

More than 1 kilogram
Less than 1 kilogram

3.

More than 1 kilogram
Less than 1 kilogram

4.

More than 1 gram
Less than 1 gram

Lesson 14-7 • Grams and Kilograms

two hundred seventy-three **273**

Practice

Circle the better estimate.

1.

More than 1 kilogram
Less than 1 kilogram

2.
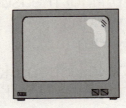

More than 1 kilogram
Less than 1 kilogram

3.

More than 1 kilogram
Less than 1 kilogram

4.
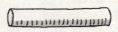

More than 1 gram
Less than 1 gram

5.

More than 1 kilogram
Less than 1 kilogram

6.

More than 1 kilogram
Less than 1 kilogram

7.

More than 1 kilogram
Less than 1 kilogram

8.

More than 1 kilogram
Less than 1 kilogram

Name _____

Lesson 14-8

Milliliters and Liters

A liter is a unit of capacity.
A milliliter is also a unit of capacity.

This bottle holds 1 liter.

A medicine dropper holds 1 milliliter.

There are 1,000 milliliters in 1 liter.
1,000 milliliters = 1 liter

Getting Started

Circle the better estimate.

1.

(More than 1 milliliter)
Less than 1 milliliter

2.

More than 1 liter
Less than 1 liter

3.

More than 1 liter
Less than 1 liter

4.

More than 1 liter
Less than 1 liter

Lesson 14-8 • Milliliters and Liters

two hundred seventy-five **275**

Practice

Circle the better estimate.

1.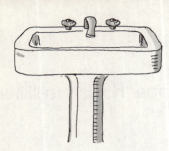

   About 20 liters
   About 200 liters

2.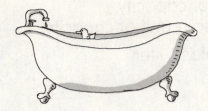

   About 200 milliliters
   About 200 liters

3.

   More than 1 liter
   Less than 1 liter

4.

   About 100 milliliters
   About 100 liters

5.

   About 2 liters
   About 20 liters

6.

   More than 1 liter
   Less than 1 liter

7.

   About 20 liters
   About 2,000 liters

8.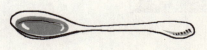

   About 5 milliliters
   About 5 liters

Name _____

Lesson 14-9

Perimeter

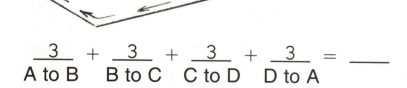

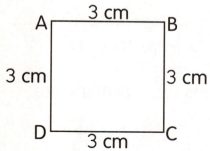

$\dfrac{3}{\text{A to B}} + \dfrac{3}{\text{B to C}} + \dfrac{3}{\text{C to D}} + \dfrac{3}{\text{D to A}} = \_\_\_$

The distance around the figure is ____ centimeters.

Getting Started

Use your centimeter ruler. Find the perimeter of each figure.

1.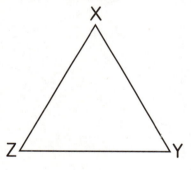

$\dfrac{\_\_\_}{\text{X to Y}} + \dfrac{\_\_\_}{\text{Y to Z}} + \dfrac{\_\_\_}{\text{Z to X}} = \_\_\_$

The perimeter is ____ centimeters.

2.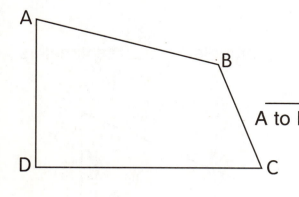

$\dfrac{\_\_\_}{\text{A to B}} + \dfrac{\_\_\_}{\text{B to C}} + \dfrac{\_\_\_}{\text{C to D}} + \dfrac{\_\_\_}{\text{D to A}} = \_\_\_$

The perimeter is ____ centimeters.

3.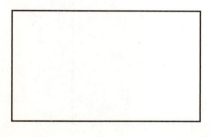

perimeter = ____ centimeters

4.

perimeter = ____ centimeters

Lesson 14-9 • Perimeter

Practice

Use your centimeter ruler.
Find the perimeter of each figure.

1.

   ___ + ___ + ___ + ___ + ___ + ___ = ___
   R to S S to T T to U U to V V to W W to R

   The perimeter is ___ centimeters.

2.

   perimeter = ___ centimeters

3.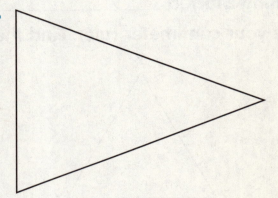

   perimeter = ___ centimeters

4.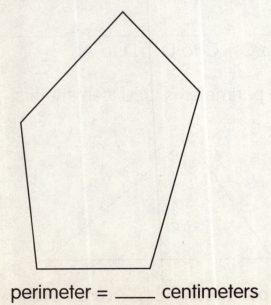

   perimeter = ___ centimeters

5.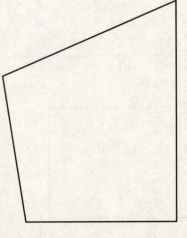

   perimeter = ___ centimeters

278 two hundred seventy-eight

Lesson 14-9 • Perimeter

Name _____

Problem Solving
Lesson 14-10

It's Algebra!

Problem Solving: Try, Check, and Revise

The perimeter of the square below is 8 centimeters. What is the length of each side?

What do I know?

The perimeter is centimeters.

A square has ____ equal sides.

Try 1	**Try 2**	**Try 3**
1 + 1 + 1 + 1 = 4. 4 is less than 8. Too small.	3 + 3 + 3 + 3 = 12 12 is greater than 8. Too big.	2 + 2 + 2 + 2 = 8 8 is equal to 8. Each side has a length of 2 centimeters.

Try, check, and revise to solve.

1. The perimeter of the triangle is 12 centimeters.

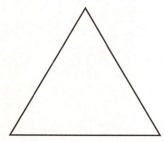

Each side of the triangle is the same length.

How long is each side?

____ centimeters

2. The perimeter of the square is 12 centimeters.

How long is each side?

____ centimeters

Lesson 14-10 • Problem Solving: Try, Check, and Revise

Practice

Try, check, and revise to solve.

1. The triangle has a perimeter of 18 centimeters. Each side is the same length.

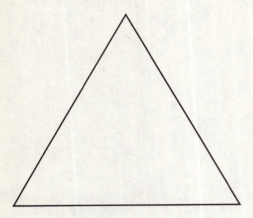

   How long is each side?
   _____ centimeters

2. The square has a perimeter of 20 centimeters.

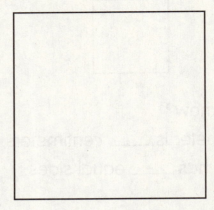

   How long is each side?
   _____ centimeters

3. The rectangle has a perimeter of 16 centimeters. The longer side has a length of 5 centimeters.

   What is the length of each of the shorter sides?
   _____ centimeters

4. The triangle has a perimeter of 9 inches. Each side of the triangle is the same length.

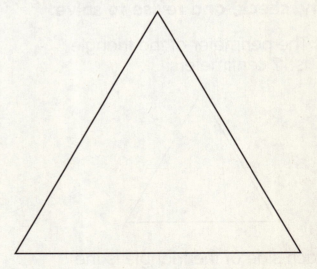

   How long is each side?
   _____ inches

Name _____

Lesson 14-11

Area

This is a square centimeter.

I can count squares to find area.

The area of this figure is ____ square centimeters.

Getting Started

Find the area of each figure.

1.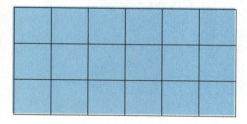

   ____ square centimeters

2.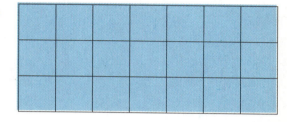

   ____ square centimeters

3.

   ____ square centimeters

4.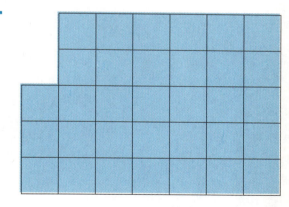

   ____ square centimeters

5.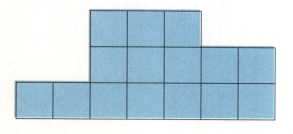

   ____ square centimeters

6.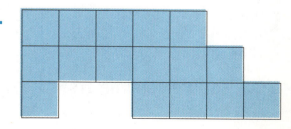

   ____ square centimeters

Lesson 14-11 • Area

two hundred eighty-one **281**

Practice

Find the area of each figure.

1.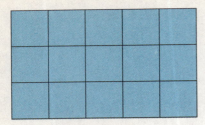
   ____ square centimeters

2.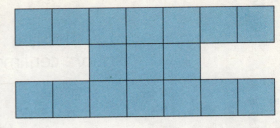
   ____ square centimeters

3.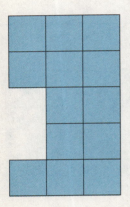
   ____ square centimeters

4.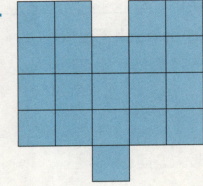
   ____ square centimeters

5.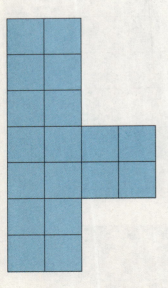
   ____ square centimeters

6.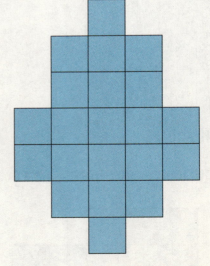
   ____ square centimeters

Name _____

Lesson 14-12

Temperature

Thermometers are used to measure temperature. This is a Fahrenheit thermometer.

This is a Celsius thermometer. It measures temperature using a different scale.

70°F   20°C

We read this as ____ degrees Fahrenheit.

We read this as ____ degrees Celsius.

Getting Started

Write each temperature.

1. ____ °F

2. ____ °C

Lesson 14-12 • Temperature   two hundred eighty-three **283**

Practice

Write each temperature.

1.

   _____ °F   _____ °C

2.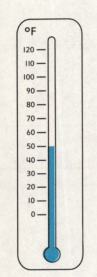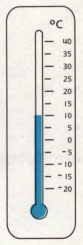

   _____ °F   _____ °C

3.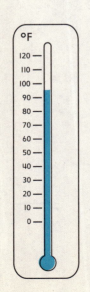

   _____ °F   _____ °C

Lesson 14-12 • Temperature

Name _____

Chapter 14 Test

Estimate the length to the nearest inch.

1.

It is between ___ and ___ inches.   ___
                                    nearest inch

Estimate the length to the nearest centimeter.

2.

It is between ___ and ___ centimeters.   ___
                                         nearest centimeter

Use your centimeter ruler. Find the perimeter of the figure.

3.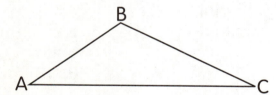

___ + ___ + ___ = ___
A to B B to C C to A

The perimeter is ___ centimeters.

Find the area.

4.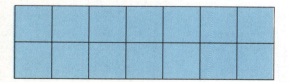

area = ___ square centimeters

Circle the better estimate.

5.

5 ounces   5 pounds

6.

1 cup   1 quart

Write the temperature.

7.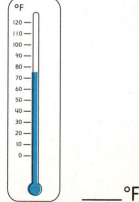

___ °F

Chapter 14 • Test

two hundred eighty-five **285**

Cumulative Assessment

Circle the letter of the correct answer.

1. 7
   + 5

   a. 2
   b. 12
   c. 13
   d. NG

2. 17 − 8

   a. 8
   b. 25
   c. 11
   d. NG

3.
   a. 365
   b. 356
   c. 653
   d. NG

4. 38
   + 96

   a. 124
   b. 62
   c. 134
   d. NG

5. 346
   + 275

   a. 621
   b. 611
   c. 511
   d. NG

6. 75 − 49

   a. 26
   b. 34
   c. 36
   d. NG

7. 524
   − 135

   a. 499
   b. 411
   c. 389
   d. NG

8. Name this shape.

   a. square
   b. rectangle
   c. triangle
   d. NG

9. What part is blue?

   a. $\frac{2}{3}$
   b. $\frac{1}{3}$
   c. $\frac{2}{4}$
   d. NG

10. 3 pints = ___?___ cups

    a. 2
    b. 6
    c. 4
    d. NG

11. What part is blue?

    a. $\frac{3}{4}$
    b. $\frac{1}{4}$
    c. $\frac{1}{3}$
    d. NG

12. Which is the better guess?

    a. more than 1 pound
    b. less than 1 pound

score

Multiplication and Division Through 5

Chapter 15

Lesson 15-1

Multiplying by the Factor 2

Rona put 2 buttons in each box. She has 4 boxes. How many buttons does she have?

(thought bubble: four 2s = ?)

We are looking for the number of buttons.

Rona put _____ buttons in each box.

She has _____ boxes.

To find the number of buttons, we can add __2__ and __2__ and __2__ and __2__, or we can multiply __2__ by __4__.

Add.

$$\begin{array}{r} 2 \\ 2 \\ 2 \\ +2 \\ \hline 8 \end{array}$$

or

Multiply.

how many in each group ↓   ↓ 2
$4 \times 2 = 8$ $\begin{array}{r} 2 \\ \times 4 \\ \hline 8 \end{array}$
↑ how many groups

Rona has _____ buttons.

Getting Started

Use different ways to find the number of buttons.

1.

   $2 + 2 + 2 =$ _____

   three 2s = _____

   $3 \times 2 =$ _____

Multiply.

2. $\begin{array}{r} 2 \\ \times 4 \\ \hline \end{array}$ 3. $\begin{array}{r} 2 \\ \times 2 \\ \hline \end{array}$ 4. $\begin{array}{r} 2 \\ \times 1 \\ \hline \end{array}$

Practice

Use different ways to find the number of buttons.

1.
   2 + 2 + 2 + 2 = ___

   four 2s = ___

   4 × 2 = ___

2.
   one 2 = ___

   1 × 2 = ___

3.
   2 + 2 = ___

   two 2s = ___

   2 × 2 = ___

4.
   2 + 2 + 2 + 2 + 2 = ___

   five 2s = ___

   5 × 2 = ___

5.
   2 + 2 + 2 = ___

   three 2s = ___

   3 × 2 = ___

Multiply.

6. 2 × 2 = ___   7. 3 × 2 = ___   8. 1 × 2 = ___

9. 4 × 2 = ___   10. 5 × 2 = ___   11. 4 × 2 = ___

12. 2   13. 2   14. 2   15. 2   16. 2
    ×2   ×4   ×1   ×3   ×5
    ---   ---   ---   ---   ---

Name _____

Lesson 15-2

Multiplying by the Factor 3

Luke put 3 pictures on each card.
He has 2 cards. How many pictures did he use?

two 3s = ?

We are looking for the number of pictures.

There are ____ pictures on each card.

There are ____ cards.

To find the number of pictures, we can add ____ and ____, or we can multiply ____ by ____.

Add.

$$\begin{array}{r} 3 \\ + 3 \\ \hline 6 \end{array}$$

Multiply.

how many in each group

$$2 \times 3 = 6 \qquad \begin{array}{r} 3 \\ \times 2 \\ \hline 6 \end{array}$$

how many groups

Luke has ____ pictures.

Getting Started

Use different ways to find the number of pictures.

1.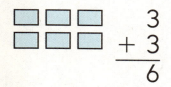

   $3 + 3 + 3 =$ ____

   three 3s = ____

   $3 \times 3 =$ ____

Multiply.

2. $\begin{array}{r} 3 \\ \times 1 \\ \hline \end{array}$ 3. $\begin{array}{r} 3 \\ \times 3 \\ \hline \end{array}$ 4. $\begin{array}{r} 3 \\ \times 2 \\ \hline \end{array}$

Lesson 15-2 • Multiplying by the Factor 3

two hundred eighty-nine **289**

Practice

Use different ways to find the number of stickers.

1.  four 3s = ___

   3 + 3 + 3 + 3 = ___   4 × 3 = ___

2.

   one 3 = ___

   1 × 3 = ___

3.

   3 + 3 + 3 = ___

   three 3s = ___

   3 × 3 = ___

4.

   3 + 3 + 3 + 3 + 3 = ___

   five 3s = ___

   5 × 3 = ___

5.

   3 + 3 = ___

   two 3s = ___

   2 × 3 = ___

Multiply.

6. 3 × 2	7. 3 × 1	8. 2 × 2	9. 2 × 4	10. 2 × 1
11. 3 × 4	12. 3 × 5	13. 3 × 3	14. 2 × 3	15. 2 × 5

Name _____

Lesson 15-3

Multiplying by the Factor 4

Mary has 3 boxes. She put 4 shells in each box. How many shells does Mary have?

We want to know the number of shells.

There are ____ boxes.

There are ____ shells in each box.

To find the number of shells, we can add ____ and ____ and ____, or we can multiply ____ by ____.

Add.

4
4
+ 4
―――
12

Multiply.

how many in each group

$3 \times 4 = 12$ $\begin{array}{r} 4 \\ \times 3 \\ \hline 12 \end{array}$

how many groups

Marty has ____ shells.

Getting Started

Use different ways to find the number of shells.

Multiply.

1.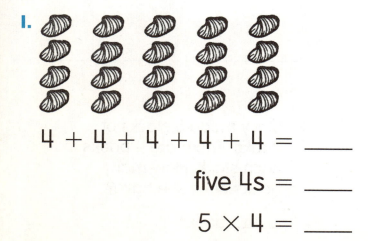

$4 + 4 + 4 + 4 + 4 =$ ____

five 4s = ____

$5 \times 4 =$ ____

2. $\begin{array}{r} 4 \\ \times 2 \\ \hline \end{array}$ 3. $\begin{array}{r} 4 \\ \times 1 \\ \hline \end{array}$ 4. $\begin{array}{r} 4 \\ \times 5 \\ \hline \end{array}$

Lesson 15-3 • Multiplying by the Factor 4

Practice

Use different ways to find the number of shells.

1.

   $4 + 4 + 4 + 4 = $ ___

   four 4s = ___

   $4 \times 4 = $ ___

2. $4 + 4 = $ ___

   two 4s = ___

   $2 \times 4 = $ ___

3. one 4 = ___

   $1 \times 4 = $ ___

Multiply.

4. $3 \times 2 = $ ___
5. $2 \times 2 = $ ___
6. $1 \times 3 = $ ___

7. $4 \times 3 = $ ___
8. $4 \times 5 = $ ___
9. $4 \times 2 = $ ___

10. $\begin{array}{r} 3 \\ \times\, 5 \\ \hline \end{array}$
11. $\begin{array}{r} 2 \\ \times\, 5 \\ \hline \end{array}$
12. $\begin{array}{r} 3 \\ \times\, 3 \\ \hline \end{array}$
13. $\begin{array}{r} 4 \\ \times\, 1 \\ \hline \end{array}$
14. $\begin{array}{r} 4 \\ \times\, 4 \\ \hline \end{array}$

Problem Solving

Solve.

15. A farm has 3 pens. There are 4 pigs in each pen. How many pigs are there?

    ___ pigs

16. Stacy made 5 stacks of books. There are 4 books in each stack. How many books does she have?

    ___ books

Lesson 15-4

Multiplying by the Factor 5

Pablo has 4 bags. He put 5 rocks in each bag. How many rocks does Pablo have?

We are looking for the number of rocks.

There are ____ bags.

There are ____ rocks in each bag.

To find the number of rocks, we can add ____ and ____ and ____ and ____, or we can multiply ____ by ____.

Add.

○○○○○   5
○○○○○   5
○○○○○   5
○○○○○ + 5
          ——
          20

Multiply.

how many in each group

$4 \times 5 = 20$ $\begin{array}{r} 5 \\ \times 4 \\ \hline 20 \end{array}$

how many groups

Pablo has ____ rocks.

Getting Started

Use different ways to find the number of rocks.

1. $5 + 5 + 5 =$ ____
    three 5s = ____
    $3 \times 5 =$ ____

Multiply.

2. $\begin{array}{r} 5 \\ \times 2 \\ \hline \end{array}$ 3. $\begin{array}{r} 5 \\ \times 1 \\ \hline \end{array}$ 4. $\begin{array}{r} 5 \\ \times 4 \\ \hline \end{array}$

Practice

Use different ways to find the number of rocks.

1.

   five 5s = ___

   5 + 5 + 5 + 5 + 5 = ___   5 × 5 = ___

2.

   one 5 = ___

   1 × 5 = ___

3.

   5 + 5 = ___

   two 5s = ___

   2 × 5 = ___

Multiply.

4. 2 × 5 = ___   5. 2 × 2 = ___   6. 4 × 5 = ___

7. 3 × 4 = ___   8. 3 × 5 = ___   9. 3 × 3 = ___

10. 1 × 2 = ___   11. 2 × 4 = ___   12. 5 × 4 = ___

13. 4 × 3 = ___   14. 5 × 5 = ___   15. 3 × 2 = ___

16. 2   17. 5   18. 4   19. 3   20. 2   21. 5
   ×2   ×4   ×2   ×3   ×5   ×5

22. 4   23. 5   24. 5   25. 2   26. 5   27. 4
   ×3   ×2   ×3   ×4   ×1   ×4

Name _____

Lesson 15-5

Order in Multiplication

Here is an important idea that makes multiplication easy.

We can multiply in any order. The answers will always be the same.

two 3s   three 2s
2 × 3 = 6   3 × 2 = 6

Getting Started

Multiply.

1. 3 × 4 = ____
   4 × 3 = ____

2. 2 × 5 = ____
   5 × 2 = ____

3. 2 × 4 = ____
   4 × 2 = ____

4. 1 × 3 = ____
   3 × 1 = ____

5.   2   3
   × 3   × 2

6.   5   4
   × 4   × 5

7.   3   5
   × 5   × 3

Find each total cost.

8.    3¢
        2   × 2

   Total cost ____

9.    2¢
        3   × 3

   Total cost ____

Practice

Multiply.

1. $5 \times 4 =$ ___
   $4 \times 5 =$ ___

2. $1 \times 5 =$ ___
   $5 \times 1 =$ ___

3. $4 \times 1 =$ ___
   $1 \times 4 =$ ___

4. $3 \times 5 =$ ___
   $5 \times 3 =$ ___

5. $\begin{array}{r} 5 \\ \times 2 \\ \hline \end{array}$ $\begin{array}{r} 2 \\ \times 5 \\ \hline \end{array}$

6. $\begin{array}{r} 4 \\ \times 2 \\ \hline \end{array}$ $\begin{array}{r} 2 \\ \times 4 \\ \hline \end{array}$

7. $\begin{array}{r} 3 \\ \times 4 \\ \hline \end{array}$ $\begin{array}{r} 4 \\ \times 3 \\ \hline \end{array}$

Find each total cost.

8. 5

   Total cost ____

9. 3

   Total cost ____

10. 3

    Total cost ____

11. 4

    Total cost ____

12. 4

    Total cost ____

13. 5

    Total cost ____

Problem Solving: Choose an Operation

Solve.

1. 2 chairs have _____ legs.
2. 5 chairs have _____ legs.
3. 3 chairs have _____ legs.
4. 4 chairs have _____ legs.

5. 3 birds have _____ legs.
6. 1 bird has _____ legs.
7. 2 birds have _____ legs.
8. 5 birds have _____ legs.
9. 4 birds have _____ legs.

10. 2 hands have _____ fingers.
11. 4 hands have _____ fingers.
12. 3 hands have _____ fingers.
13. 1 hand has _____ fingers.
14. 5 hands have _____ fingers.

Practice

Write a multiplication sentence for each. Solve.

1.

   How many buttons are there in all?

   $2 \times 4 = 8$

   There are ____ buttons.

2.

   How many birds are there in all?

   _____

   There are ____ birds.

3.

   How many flowers are there in all?

   _____

   There are ____ flowers.

4.

   How many tires are there in all?

   _____

   There are ____ tires.

5.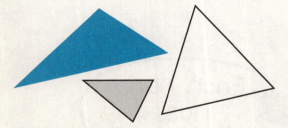

   How many sides are there in all?

   _____

   There are ____ sides.

6.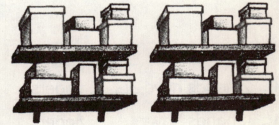

   How many boxes are there in all?

   _____

   There are ____ boxes.

Name _____

Lesson 15-7

Dividing by 2

It's Algebra!

There are 10 children at the playground. They are going to form 2 teams. How many children will be on each team?

To find the answer, we can use counters to make equal groups.

We can find how many children will be on each team by dividing 10 by 2. The division sentence is 10 ÷ 2.

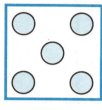

10 ÷ 2 = 5
How many in all? How many groups? How many in each group?

There will be __5__ children on each team.

Getting Started

Draw a picture to show equal groups.

1. 8 pennies in two equal groups

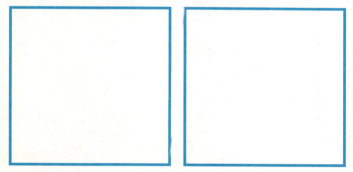

2. 6 crayons in two equal groups

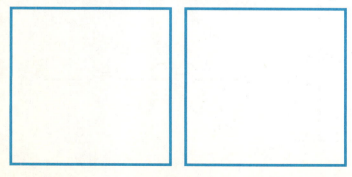

Lesson 15-7 • Dividing by 2

two hundred ninety-nine **299**

Practice

**Draw a picture to show equal groups.
Then write a division sentence for each.**

1. 8 cupcakes divided between 2 boxes

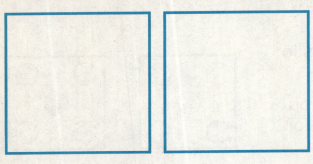

___8___ ÷ ___2___ = ___4___

2. 2 slices of pizza divided between 2 plates

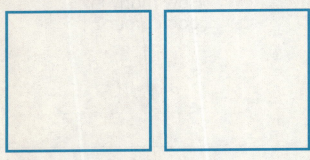

_____ ÷ _____ = _____

3. 10 people divided between 2 cars

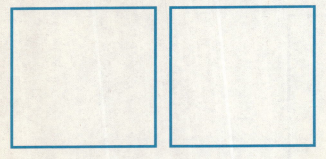

_____ ÷ _____ = _____

4. 6 cookies divided between 2 plates

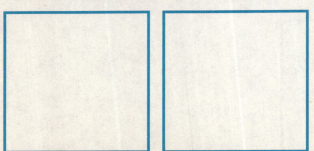

_____ ÷ _____ = _____

Lesson 15-8

Dividing by 3

It's Algebra!

Lonnie has 15 cookies to give to 3 friends. How many cookies will each friend get?

You can put counters into equal groups to find the answer.

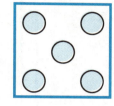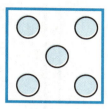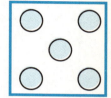

We can find how many cookies each friend will get by dividing 15 by 3. The division sentence is 15 ÷ 3.

15 ÷ 3 = 5

How many in all?   How many groups?   How many in each group?

Each friend will get ___5___ cookies.

Getting Started

Draw a picture to show equal groups.

1. 9 cats in three equal groups

2. 6 pencils in three equal groups

Practice

**Draw a picture to show equal groups.
Then write a division sentence for each.**

1. 3 pies divided among 3 boxes

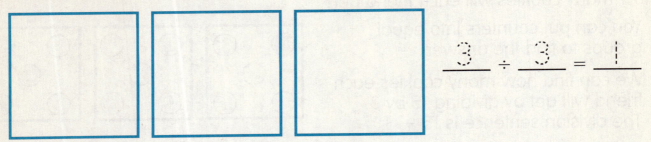

$\underline{3} \div \underline{3} = \underline{1}$

2. 12 slices of pizza divided among 3 plates

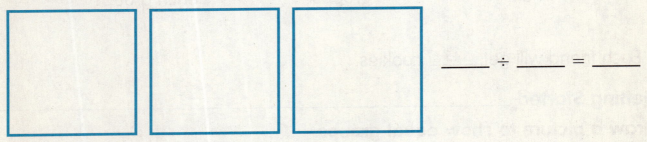

$\underline{} \div \underline{} = \underline{}$

3. 9 quarters divided among 3 groups

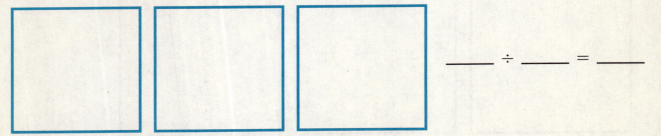

$\underline{} \div \underline{} = \underline{}$

4. 15 hats divided among 3 groups

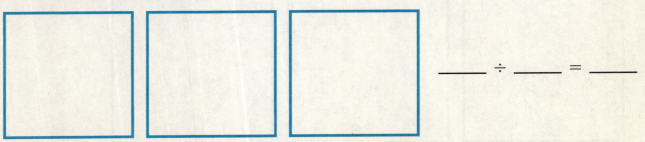

$\underline{} \div \underline{} = \underline{}$

Lesson 15-9

Name _____

Dividing by 4

It's Algebra!

Josh has 16 quarters. 4 quarters are equal to 1 dollar. How many dollars does Josh have?

To find the answer, use quarters to make equal groups.

We can find how many dollars Josh has by dividing 16 by 4. The division sentence is 16 ÷ 4.

$$16 \div 4 = \underline{4}$$

How many quarters in all?   How many quarters in a dollar?   How many dollars?

Josh has __4__ dollars.

Getting Started

Draw a picture to show equal groups.

1. 12 marbles in four equal groups

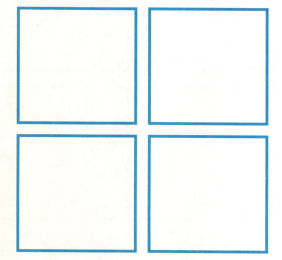

2. 8 crayons in four equal groups

Practice

**Draw a picture to show equal groups.
Then write a division sentence for each.**

1. 4 cookies divided among 4 plates

___4___ ÷ ___4___ = ___1___

2. 16 pencils divided among 4 boxes

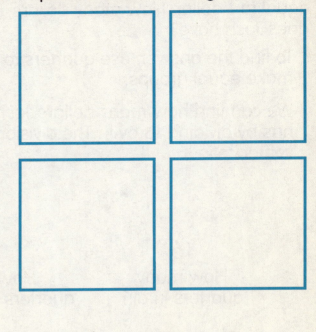

_____ ÷ _____ = _____

3. 20 dogs divided among 4 groups

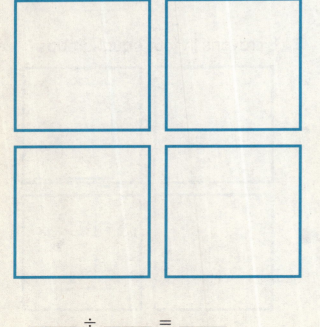

_____ ÷ _____ = _____

4. 8 cupcakes divided among 4 boxes

_____ ÷ _____ = _____

Name _____

Lesson 15-10

Dividing by 5

It's Algebra!

There are 20 children playing basketball at the gym. There are 5 teams. How many children are on a team?

To find the answer, use counters to make equal groups.

We can find how many children are on each team by dividing 20 by 5. The division sentence is 20 ÷ 5.

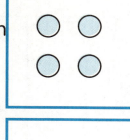
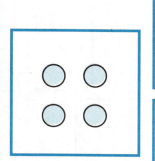
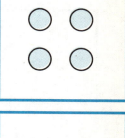

20 ÷ 5 = __4__
How many in all?   How many groups?   How many in each group?

There are __4__ children on each team.

Getting Started

Draw a picture to show equal groups.

1. 10 dimes in five equal groups

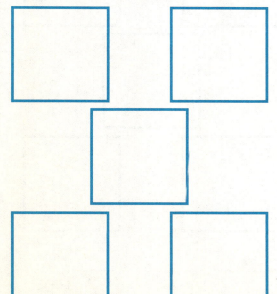

2. 5 stars in five equal groups

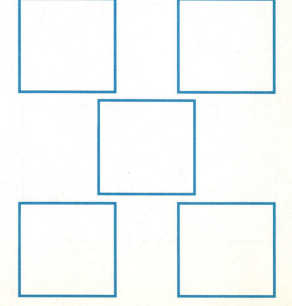

Lesson 15-10 • Dividing by 5   three hundred five **305**

Practice

**Draw a picture to show equal groups.
Then write a division sentence for each.**

1. 20 crayons divided among 5 boxes

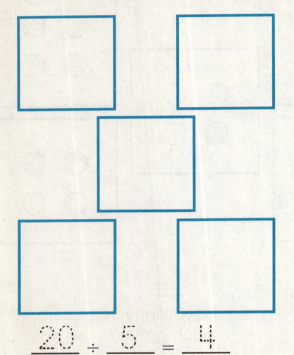

__20__ ÷ __5__ = __4__

2. 15 pencils divided among 5 boxes

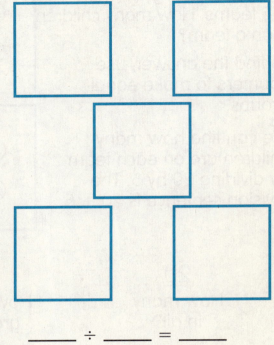

_____ ÷ _____ = _____

3. 25 buttons divided among 5 groups

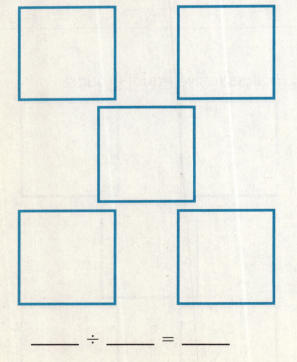

_____ ÷ _____ = _____

4. 5 slices of pizza divided among 5 plates

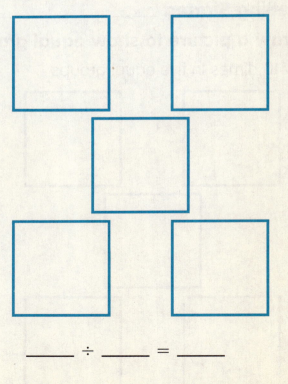

_____ ÷ _____ = _____

Problem Solving: Make and Use a Picture Graph

Mary made a picture graph to show the books she read in January. Another name for a picture graph is pictograph.

Books Read in January	
First week	📖 📖
Second week	📖 📖 📖 📖
Third week	📖 📖 📖
Fourth week	📖 📖 📖 📖 📖

Each 📖 stands for 2 books.

How many books did Mary read

the first week? __4__

the second week? _____

the third week? _____

the fourth week? _____

Getting Started

Write each answer on the lines.

1. Mary read the most books during the _____ week.

2. She read the fewest books during the _____ week.

3. How many more books did Mary read the fourth week than the first week?

   _____ − _____ = _____

4. How many books did Mary read the first two weeks?

   _____ + _____ = _____

Practice

5 children made a tally of the shells they found at the beach.

Color the number of shells to show how many shells each child found.

1. Del
2. Jennifer
3. Rosa
4. Joseph
5. Rodney

Each 🐚 stands for 5 shells.

Answer each question.

6. Who found the most shells? _____

7. Who found the fewest shells? _____

8. How many shells were found by Del and Jennifer? ____

9. How many shells were found by Joseph and Rodney? ____

10. How many more shells were found by Rosa than Rodney? ____

Coordinate Graph

Lesson 15-12
It's Algebra!

A coordinate graph is used to show where objects are located.

This graph shows where places are located in a town. Find the mall.

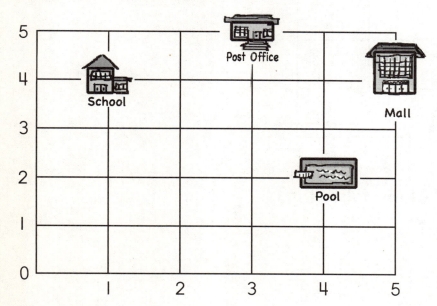

Always start at 0.

First, count to the right →. The mall is __5__ units to the right.

Then, count up ↑. The mall is ____ units up.

To find the mall, go to the right ____ and up ____.

Getting Started

Use the graph to find each of the following.

               Right →   Up ↑   Right →   Up ↑

1. School   ____   ____   2. Post Office   ____   ____

3. Mall   ____   ____   4. Pool   ____   ____

Practice

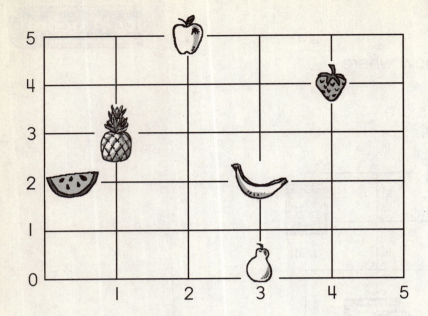

Use the graph to find each of the following.

                      Right →   Up ↑

1. 🍌   _____   _____

2. 🍎   _____   _____

3. 🍉   _____   _____

4. 🍓   _____   _____

5. 🍐   _____   _____

6. 🍍   _____   _____

Chapter 15 Test

Name _____

Multiply.

1.

   $3 \times 4 = $ ___

2.

   $2 \times 4 = $ ___

3.

   $3 \times 5 = $ ___

4.

   $5 \times 2 = $ ___

5. $\begin{array}{r} 5 \\ \times 4 \\ \hline \end{array}$
6. $\begin{array}{r} 4 \\ \times 5 \\ \hline \end{array}$
7. $\begin{array}{r} 3 \\ \times 3 \\ \hline \end{array}$
8. $\begin{array}{r} 3 \\ \times 4 \\ \hline \end{array}$
9. $\begin{array}{r} 5 \\ \times 2 \\ \hline \end{array}$

Divide.

10. $10 \div 5 = $ ___
11. $9 \div 3 = $ ___
12. $8 \div 2 = $ ___

Solve.

13. Calvin bought 3 bunches of carrots. There are 5 carrots in each bunch. How many carrots does he have?

    ___ carrots

14. There are 16 wheels. Each car has 4 wheels. How many cars are there in all?

    There are ___ cars.

Find the total cost.

15. 5

    Total cost ___

16. 3

    Total cost ___

Cumulative Assessment

Circle the letter of the correct answer.

1.   7
  + 8
      a. 16
      b. 1
      c. 15
      d. NG

2. 13 − 6
      a. 7
      b. 13
      c. 19
      d. NG

3.
      a. 3:45
      b. 8:15
      c. 8:03
      d. NG

4.
      a. 85¢
      b. 80¢
      c. 75¢
      d. NG

5.   37
  + 54
      a. 23
      b. 81
      c. 83
      d. NG

6.   356
  + 575
      a. 931
      b. 921
      c. 821
      d. NG

7.   81
  − 55
      a. 36
      b. 26
      c. 34
      d. NG

8.   623
  − 298
      a. 325
      b. 335
      c. 435
      d. NG

9. What part of the figure is blue?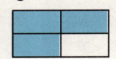
      a. $\frac{2}{4}$
      b. $\frac{1}{4}$
      c. $\frac{3}{4}$
      d. NG

10.   5
  × 3
      a. 8
      b. 15
      c. 2
      d. NG

11. $8.35
  − 4.26
      a. $4.11
      b. $4.19
      c. $4.09
      d. NG

12. 8 ÷ 4
      a. 1
      b. 2
      c. 3
      d. NG

score

STOP

Glossary

A

add to put numbers together to find the total amount; for example, 2 + 4 = 6

after next; for example, 45 is after 44.

area the amount of space in a figure

B

bar graph a graph that compares the number of two or more objects

before ahead of; for example, 44 is before 45.

C

calendar a table that shows the days, weeks, and months of a given year

cent (¢) one penny

centimeter (cm) a metric unit of length

congruent figures figures that are exactly the same size and shape

cup (c) a customary unit of capacity

cylinder a space figure with two bases that are circles

D

day 24 hours

degrees (°) units used to measure temperature

digit any one of the ten number symbols: 0, 1, 2, 3, 4, 5, 6, 7, 8, 9

dime a coin that is worth 10 cents

dollar ($) paper money that is worth 100 cents

divide to separate into equal parts

dividend the number to be divided

E

edge the line where two plane faces on a solid figure meet

elapsed time the amount of time that has passed between two given times

estimate to quickly find an answer that is close to an exact answer

F

face the flat part of a solid figure

factors numbers that are multiplied

foot (ft) a unit of measurement equal to 12 inches

fraction a form of a number that shows parts of a whole

G

greater than more than; for example, 65 is greater than 33.

H

half-dollar a coin that is worth 50 cents

half-hour 30 minutes

hour 60 minutes

I

inch (in.) a customary unit of length

K

kilogram (kg) a metric unit of mass

L

length how long an object is

less than fewer than; for example, 33 is less than 65.

line of symmetry a line that divides a figure into two parts that are exactly the same

liter (L) a metric unit of capacity

M

meter (m) a metric unit of length

minute 60 seconds

mixed number a number made up of a whole number and a fraction

month a period of time equaling almost 4 weeks

multiples possible products of a given number

multiply to add a number to itself one or more times

N

nickel a coin that is worth 5 cents

O

ordinal numbers a number used to tell order or position; for example, first, second

P

perimeter the distance around a figure

pint (pt) a customary unit of capacity that is equal to 2 cups

place value hundreds, tens, or ones

pound (lb) a customary unit of weight

product the answer to a multiplication problem

Q

quart (qt) a customary unit of capacity equal to 2 pints

quarter a coin that is worth 25 cents

R

regroup (in addition) to rename and then carry a tens digit to the place on the left when adding

regroup (in subtraction) to rename and then carry a tens digit to the place on the right when subtracting

S

subtract to take away one number from another

V

vertex a point where three faces of a solid figure meet

W

week 7 days

Y

year 12 months